Painters First

MARLYSE TOVAE   *Anemones in Vase*   Oil

First Published in England 1995 by
Leader Books
Unit 3, Park Works
Kingsley
Bordon
Hampshire

ISBN 0 907159 03 6

Cover Picture: Charles Fowler *Cliff Scene* Watercolour

Photographs taken specifically for this book were by
the author and Simon Alexander

Printed by Arrowhead Printing Limited

Painters First

by Marc Alexander

LEADER BOOKS

PAST MASTERS

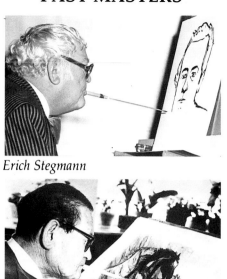
Erich Stegmann

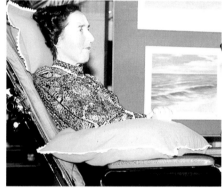
Carl Fischer

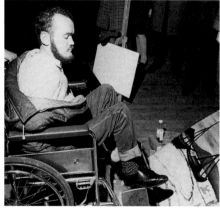
Elizabeth Twistington Higgins

Christy Brown

Alison Lapper

Charles Fowler

Florence Bunn

Heather Strudwick

Grant Sharman

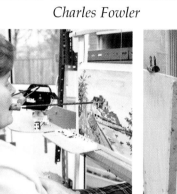
Myron Angus

Ruth Christensen

Phillip Swanepoel

Paul Driver

Nancy Rae Litteral

John Savage

Steven Chambers

José Gerado Uribe

Trevor Wells

Peter Spencer

Klaus Spahni

Tom Yendell

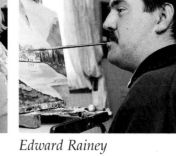
Edward Rainey

Stojan Zafred

Eros Bonamini

Jayantilal Shihora

Johnny Ang

John Bunce

Bruce Peardon

Glenn Barnett

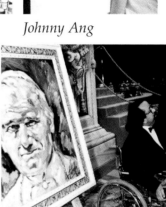
Christobal Moreno-Toledo

Iwao Adachi

Jingsheng Liu

Marlyse Tovae

Mojgan Safa

Soon-Yi Oh

Wendy Barber

Joy Clarke

Kris Kirk

Kun-Shan Hsieh

Introduction

'No pity please'

The above words were the slogan of one of the most remarkable men that this century has produced, Erich Stegmann, whose story is told in these pages. During his life he was regarded as remarkable for his ability as an artist, and now even more so for the self-help organisation he founded forty years ago.

Thanks to his inspiration and foresight, today there are over four hundred handicapped artists in fifty-eight countries who enjoy the security afforded by the international partnership known as the Association of Mouth and Foot Painting Artists.

The crucial word is 'partnership'. When Erich Stegmann conceived his plan for uniting disabled painters to enable them to live by their own creative efforts, the idea of charity was an anathema to him hence his plea of 'No pity please.' Since then the Association has striven to make it clear that it is not a charity and does not qualify for charitable assistance.

It is understandable that lay people should associate handicapped artists with charity because there are so many worthwhile charitable organisations concerned with the welfare of the disabled. It is an attitude symbolized by the fact that if Erich Stegmann was painting out-of-doors and placed his hat on the ground beside him well-intentioned people started tossing coins into it!

Members of the Association do not need charity because they are professional artists in their own right.

'What difference does it make how a picture is painted?' Erich Stegmann once said. 'A painter does not mean only a pair of hands – he paints from his heart what his eyes see... Pictures are like children who leave home. Nobody asks them whether their father has lost a foot or an arm.'

And the whole point of the Association is that its members must be of a professional standard. An independent panel of art specialists regularly reviews the work of those who have been granted AMFPA scholarships. When it is agreed that a student's work has reached a standard judged to be the equal to that of able-bodied professionals, full membership is granted.

The Association is constantly seeking new members. When contact is made with a disabled person who appears to have artistic potential his or her work is evaluated and if it is considered sufficiently promising a scholarship is offered. Students receive stipends to assist them in furthering their talents with painting materials, tuition and specially designed equipment if necessary. This may include electric wheelchairs or vans adapted to carry them which are often beyond the reach of the handicapped surviving on state benefits.

When students win the accolade of full membership they are provided with a monthly income for life regardless of whether increasing disability makes it impossible for them to continue producing paintings that can be marketed as greetings cards!

This is an outstanding feature of the Association's policy because it removes the greatest concern of the handicapped artist – the dread of losing one's ability through deteriorating health and consequently the income derived from it. The cost of living is high for the disabled – especially for those who have to pay regular helpers. A guaranteed income for life leaves the handicapped artist free to concentrate on his or her real work without being overshadowed by financial anxiety.

Perhaps the most important aspect of the Association is that it is democratically governed

ERICH STEGMANN   *Self Portrait*   Sculpture

ERICH STEGMANN   *Positano*   Oil

ERICH STEGMANN   *Fishing Boat in Burano*   Tempera

ERICH STEGMANN   *Burano*   Tempera   62 x 88 cm

by the members themselves. Under the presidency of the famous foot-painter Marlyse Tovae a board of elected delegates from different parts of the world meets at least once a year.

For electoral purposes there are four areas – Europe, Africa & The Middle East, the Americas, The Far East and Australasia & Oceania. The convention of delegates from these regions is responsible for the ultimate control of the Association's activities and, with the exception of their legal adviser, all delegates are disabled artists.

Although I have written considerably on artists of the AMFPA, I am still fascinated by these exceptional people. For one thing they are so diverse in their work, their backgrounds and the nature of their disabilities. Some have been handicapped from birth, others were able-bodied until catapulted into the world of the disabled through unexpected illness or accident. Indeed when working on this book I found that the commonest cause of injury was through diving accidents in which the lives of vigorous young men were altered irredeemably within seconds.

In these pages you will read about the lives of artists representative of the Association who have created their own worlds in form and colour for our enjoyment and inspiration. Each has his or her own style of painting, philosophy and belief but the one thing they share in common is that, no matter what handicaps destiny has laid upon them, they are all painters first.

Marc Alexander

Past Masters

'Painting became everything to me. By it I learned to express myself in many subtle ways. Through it I made articulate all that I saw and felt, all that went on inside the mind that was housed within my useless body like a prisoner in a cell looking out on a world that hadn't become a reality to me.'

So wrote Christy Brown in his famous book My Left Foot that was later made into a film of the same name which won acclaim round the world. Born in Dublin in 1932, Christy suffered from cerebral palsy which caused paralysis in his arms and legs. In his biography he described growing up in a large poverty-stricken family unable to do anything for himself, his mother being his support.

In a moving passage he told how he clenched a stick of yellow chalk – his sisters had been using it to do their sums – between the toes of his left foot and struggled to print the letter A on the floor.

'That one letter ... was my road to a new world, my key to mental freedom,' he wrote later. 'It was to provide a source of relaxation to the tense, taut thing that was me which panted for expression behind a twisted mouth.'

After this initial success he worked desperately to write with his foot. It was a highly dramatic moment in the film when the first word he managed to print was MOTHER.

As Christy grew older and mastered the technique of using his foot as a hand he turned to drawing and painting. When he was twelve the *Sunday Independent* ran a Christmas painting competition in the form of a black and white scene from Cinderella which had to be coloured in by young readers. Christy painstakingly applied the colour – and won.

This success, minor though it might have seemed to an able-bodied child, was a tremendous encouragement and from then on painting became a vital part of his life, as his words quoted at the beginning testify. In many ways he was speaking for hundreds of disabled artists who have struggled to express themselves by means of brushes gripped in their teeth or held in their toes.

In another part of the book he wrote, 'Painting became the one great love in my life, the main pivot of my concentration. I lived within the orbit of my paints and brushes.'

Christy Brown found world fame as an author and a poet – what is not generally known is that he received great assistance from the Association of Mouth and Foot Paining Artists until his unexpected death in 1981. It was the German mouth-painter Arnulf Erich Stegmann who went to Ireland to see him, finding him in a shed at his parents' home in Dublin, and invited him to join the self-help organisation he had founded in the mid-fifties.

The Association was Erich Stegmann's dream of a world partnership of disabled artists come true, a dream that had its beginnings when he was on the run from the Nazis during the Second World War. And now he sought such artists with the tireless

PIETER MOLEVELD
Dachshund
Oil   43 x 32 cm

CARL FISCHER   *Mouse Game*   Watercolour   35 x 50 cm

ELIZABETH TWISTINGTON-HIGGINS *Dancing* Oil/Papier 36 x 44 cm

PIETER MOLEVELD
Still Life with Roses
Oil

determination that radiated from him despite his own severe physical handicap. Those who met him always came away with the impression of vitality that surrounded him like a force field. Through some osmotic process he was able to infuse his confidence into those he was dedicated to helping, yet like all true confidence it was hard won.

Erich Stegmann had had to prove himself to himself again and again after he contracted poliomyelitis as a young child. Born the son of a bank clerk in Darmstadt in 1912, he was taken dangerously ill soon after the First World War broke out. The doctor broke it to his mother and father that their child was suffering from what was then known as Infantile Paralysis. As the result of the virus causing inflammation of the anterior horn cells of the spinal cord which govern muscle action it left its victims in varying degrees of paralysis.

When Erich survived the initial attack it became evident that he had lost the use of his arms and hands while his legs were also badly affected. He realized his disability when he watched his brothers and sisters romping and was powerless to join in with them.

Once in conversation with the German author J.H. Roesler, Erich told him, 'I always remember when I was five years old how my mother put me to bed because of some mischief I was up to. You see, that was the way we were punished. We were not slapped when we had done wrong, but were undressed and without any arguments or explanations were put to bed.' "You must stay in bed until I take you up!"

'The period we had to spend in bed was based on the gravity of the mischief we had done. It might be one hour or two hours. But it often happened, of course, that mother would forget to let us up again, perhaps because of the arrival of a visitor, or for some other reason. My brothers or sisters climbed out of bed themselves when their time was up but I could not stir without my mother's help – could not put on my clothes myself. Thus it turned out that I had to stay in bed beyond the time specified which I felt was most unjust! "Wicked mother! Wicked mother!" I used to rage helplessly, and it was from this experience that my resolution grew to become someone who could earn a lot of money so that I should not be dependent on anybody. This resolution, which I never gave up, made me succeed also in school.'

This thirst for independence was to remain the lodestone of Erich's life, first for himself and then for others. And at that remarkably early age he recognized that for the disabled money was the key to the things that the able-bodied took for granted – a home, a place in which to work, the means to travel, security.

When Erich was taken to school, his useless hands tucked neatly in his pockets, he sat stiffly and watched his fellow pupils working with pencils and crayons in their hands. If he felt like crying with frustration he held his tears back – his mother was not there to wipe them away. Instead he managed to manoeuvre the end of a pencil between his teeth and started trying to form his letters.

'I began to write and paint with the other children,' he recalled later in life. 'But I wanted to do better than the others. They wrote and painted with their hands – my hands were paralysed and I painted with my mouth so I wanted to prove to them that I could do it better than those who were not handicapped. And I did better. In fact I did it so well that in 1927 I was accepted into the art school at the age of fifteen, and I was allowed to do live models at the age of sixteen, a privilege seldom granted to students of that age. I worked like mad and won a scholarship from the Lord

Mayor of Nuremberg, where my parents now lived, to work for one year in the studio of a famous artist. The choice was left to me and I went to Erwin von Kormendy, a Hungarian painter.'

With each success Erich's confidence increased and by the time he was twenty-two he felt able to leave home. He shared a studio with his brother-in-law and set about earning his living as a professional painter. The life of an artist was something he had often imagined as a boy, and now it was made all the more sweet by his relationship with a girl named Bobby Hartman who was later to become his wife. Well aware that painting, like all forms of artistic expression, is not usually a safe profession from the financial standpoint, he set up his own publishing house.

But even the art world found it impossible to ignore politics in the 'thirties. It was a time of tension and stress, some feared the Communists and others the National Socialists led by the failed painter Adolf Hitler who, ten years after he was imprisoned for leading and unsuccessful rising in Munich, became the Chancellor.

From the start Erich Stegmann, with his fierce belief in individual freedom, was opposed to the Nazis and never failed to give tongue to his opposition. This made him officially an 'enemy of the state', and as such he was arrested at the end of 1934.

For the next fifteen months he had to endure gaol, not an easy situation for the able-bodied but ghastly for someone so physically handicapped, and as a piece of extra malice he was not allowed his paints. The result was that his physical condition deteriorated so badly that the medical officer responsible for the local prison decided that he should be transferred to the Munich prison at Ettstrasse which would not be such a strain on his health. And it was at Ettstrasse that he had an unexpected birthday present – the case against him was abandoned for lack of evidence. Years later he was to become an honorary member of the board of directors of an organization representing those who had been persecuted during the Nazi period – the Vereinigung der Verfolgten des Naziregimes.

Two months after his release he married Bobby and returned to publishing and painting. His experience of gaol did not deter him from continuing to oppose the Nazi Party and in 1944 he was forced to flee into hiding until the end of the Second World War. It was also the time that he and Bobby – with whom he shared two children – found that their marriage did not work.

In the chaos of early post-war Germany Erich sought to re-establish both his professional and private life. Some time after his divorce he married Traudi Millmeir, with whom he had two more children. He returned to painting and in the 'fifties was having one-man exhibitions in various capital cities.

Once when told how in a Rome art gallery the proprietor made a point of telling customers that his pictures exhibited there had been painted by mouth, Erich exploded, 'What difference does it make how a picture is painted? A painter does not mean only a pair of hands – he paints from his heart what his eyes see. The picture then wants to find friends. Pictures are like children who leave home. Nobody asks them whether their father has lost a foot or an arm. Whey then should it arise with my pictures?'

Soon after the war Erich had 'discovered' the Adriatic island of Burano, a short boat-ride from Venice, which is noted for its traditional lace-making and old Venetian-style buildings. These houses with their vivid reflections trembling in the lagoon were an inspiration which brought him back to the island year after year. He bought a plot of land there and parked a caravan on it which became his summer

CHRISTY BROWN *Winter Landscape* Oil

PETER SPENCER *Abersoch Harbour*

residence. The view of him sitting in front of his easel, brush in mouth, became one of the commonplace sights of the island, and the only thing that may have struck the passers-by as odd was that he was the best-dressed artist ever to come to Venice.

In the beginning Erich painted out-of-doors as he did in his studio, in old comfortable clothing that was paint-spattered and gave off the smell of turps. One day when sitting at his easel to paint a street scene a crowd of instant art critics gathered round him as people will round an artist to see how close his or her painting is to the subject, and it was seen that this artist – Good heavens! he has to paint with his mouth! – had his hat on the ground beside him. To the sympathetic onlookers this meant only one thing – and coins tinkled into the hat.

Although Erich perfectly understood their motives he felt he could not stand being the object of charity.

'Most people are so extremely considerate, they believe I am dependent on their help,' he said. 'That drives me mad.'

However, he had to face the fact that if he sat at his easel in public in his comfortable studio clothes the well-intended coins would continue to rain about him. His solution was to paint wearing a very expensive suit, the finest shirt money could buy and a bow tie. From then on no one dared to offer a coin to this personification of sartorial elegance.

It is an amusing anecdote but it also illustrates Erich Stegmann's fundamental attitude which became the keystone of the Association of Mouth and Foot Painting Artists, the last thing he wanted was for people to think of it as a charity – it was to be a partnership.

Erich knew only too well the problems besetting disabled paints, many of whom were more disabled than he who could at least walk, and one of the main ones was the difficulty in making a living through artistic endeavour. Others, he knew, had the potential to become artists but were without the means to afford training or even in some cases the cost of paints, brushes and canvases. But with a partnership based on mutual help, and with a proper marketing programme, he believed correctly that it was possible for such artists to be self-supporting.

In 1956 Erich Stegmann launched the Association of Mouth and Foot Painting Artists.

Its inaugural meeting took place in March of the following year at the Waldhotel in Vaduz, Liechtenstein. Seventeen founder members assembled for the first General Meeting of the Association at which its statutes were signed – a key resolution stating that the AMFPA must be neutral from a religious, ideological or political viewpoint, thus 'any preference or prejudice because of the religious, ideological or political beliefs of a member is not therefore permissible.'

Despite his work as President and Founder of the Association, Erich Stegmann continued with his own art and when one looks at his work one is amazed at the variety of talent. There are his famous Burano paintings with their hot ochres, dark reds and greens and washed-out blues which immediately make one nostalgic for Venice. In contrast there are his delicate water-colours, his surreal works and abstracts, and his seemingly primitive works which radiate the strength of their creator.

He loved to experiment with every technique possible, ranging from litho work to prints made from wood blocks he incised with mouth-held tools. And, remarkable as it may seem, he used the same method with chisels to carve wood.

Erich Stegmann achieved the independent life that was his goal as a child, yet as well as success he experienced tragedy – the two children of his first marriage died in road accidents five years apart. He died in 1984 but, like John Brown in the American Civil War song, his spirit marches on. His inspiration is there every time a student or member of the Association he founded takes a brush in his or her teeth or toes.

When Erich Stegmann set up the Association of Mouth and Foot Painting Artists he knew that, if the scheme was to succeed, it would be essential to have members who could provide paintings for greeting cards that would equal, and indeed surpass, those already on the market. The last thing he wanted to do was publish work that would be bought out of pity – pity was an anathema to him. His aim was to help disabled artists, or those with artistic potential, to become self-sufficient but they had to be artists whose work was as competent as their able-bodied counterparts. There was no room in the Association for those without talent.

While there were a number of handicapped painters who would achieve a high enough standard after tuition, which in some cases might take several years, the Association needed artists already proficient to supply the artwork that would lay the foundations for the enterprise. And it is thanks to the efforts of these original few that so many disabled artists are able to live by the brush today.

One of the great pioneers of mouth painting was Elof Lundberg who became the first Scandinavian member of the AMFPA in 1956. Though his was one of the Association's foremost success stories, few guessed when they met this genial man, with a distinctive streak of white in his hair, at the horror of his early life and the despair that it fostered.

Imagine this scene: a freezing December morning in Stockholm. A nurse draws back a dormitory curtain and sees on the terrace what looks like a statue amid the whirling snowflakes. She shouts for help and then dashes outside to find it is a youth in his nightshirt who had been crouched out there for three hours with tears frozen on his cheeks ... Elof Lundberg was trying to end his life which had become unbearable.

He was carried into a room where a doctor watched over him day and night, trying to bring him back from the twilight border between life and death. At last he began to recover from the effects of exposure until the kindly doctor said, 'We will take you back to your parents tomorrow, Elof.'

He had naturally expected the patients reaction to be one of delight and he was shocked when he started up in bed, sweating and his eyes staring in terror.

'Not to my parents – anywhere else but not to my parents!' What lay behind that heartfelt cry can best be told in Elof Lundberg's own words. He had been born in 1917, one of eight children of a metal polisher and his wife. Of these three died a week after their birth and the sickly infant Elof had been expected to follow them.

'It was thanks to a hard smack on my behind that I lived and for many years later I thought it would have been better had I been allowed to die,' he recalled in Stockholm soon after he had become a member of the AMFPA. 'Nobody cared about me and I was allowed to lie around the house unnoticed. My mother, who had no time for anything weak or unhealthy, did not like me.

'She apparently forgot that I was her own flesh and blood and she would have preferred that I had been born dead or that I should have died within days of my birth as had three of my sisters. Four of the children grew up healthy and strong and filled the house with merriment but I, the invalid child, lay around a helpless bundle, a bother to all, crippled, squint-eyed and unable to stir.'

Elof was six years old when life suddenly changed for the better. He was put into an establishment that combined schooling and nursing known as the Eugenia Home. Here the crippled child found himself amid the camaraderie of the disabled – here he was able to feel normal.

At the home he was taught reading and writing and after attempts to get him to hold a pencil in his hand failed he tried holding it in his mouth. It was a matter of great pride to him that after three years he had the best 'handwriting' in the class. Drawing by the same method followed.

During this period Elof underwent surgery in an attempt to put his twisted arms into a normal position while his feet were broken so that they could be reset – an operation that was repeated eight times. This, at least, was successful in that Elof was able finally to walk like a non-disabled person though he never gained the use of his arms. In all he underwent twenty operations.

When it seemed that nothing more could be done for him at the Eugenia Home it was decided that the time had come for Elof to return to his parents' home.

Now that he could walk the boy looked forward to going home. As he put it, 'I was able to run and was so different from the crippled little being I had been.'

His feeling of elation as he set out with a nurse was destined to be short-lived.

Looking back on that moment, Elof said, 'Neither my mother nor my father had ever come to visit me and when I arrived home – it was a Thursday, I remember well, and the day after my fifteenth birthday – my mother did not want to take me in and the nurse who was in charge of me had to insist that she should do so. No sooner had the nurse left, however, that my mother kicked me and shouted, "I don't want to nurse him! I don't want to see him! I hate him!" My father, who afterwards left her, was too weak to stand up for me.'

The days that followed were, to quote Elof again, 'full of blows and curses'.

Finally he was placed in another institution, but what a difference it was to the Eugenia Home where his legs had been cured and he had learned to draw with a mouth-held pencil.

In his new surrounds Elof was put into a ward that was set aside for hopeless cases because there was no one to pay for him to have better accommodation.

'The nights were horrible,' he recalled. 'There were forty of us in one dormitory, young and old, and during the nights many of the patients used to run around the room and annoy the others. In the mornings many patients would be found lying on the floor, their limbs rigid, some of them even dead, after having been thrown out of their beds during the night by some of the insane inmates. For three years I lived in this hell....'

There came the night when he could stand it no longer and he decided to end his life – his third attempt at suicide.

At 4 a.m. young Elof stole out on to the terrace and waited for the intense cold to end his misery. He had just turned eighteen.

After the compassionate doctor, who had brought him back to health, realized the boy's anguish Elof was allowed to have a room to himself and in order to improve his physical condition he had a series of operations on his eyes.

A year passed following his suicide attempt and then, when nothing further could be done for him medically, he was told that he must leave his room to make way for the next patient requiring attention.

Thus at nineteen Elof Lundberg found himself out on the street, alone and afraid, and without income or home. He found himself an inexpensive room with a kindly old lady who, being poor herself, needed the rent money to survive. Although she treated him with great kindness, Elof realized the necessity of paying his rent regularly and looked about for ways to make money. The one talent he had was for painting and he took to painting postcards which he sold for small amounts in cafes. As his technique improved he even sold a few still life pictures.

He worked long hours on his postcards, earning only just enough to survive, but was plagued by the thought that it was because of his disability rather than talent that induced people to buy his work.

And then he realized that he had a second talent. He had a find baritone voice and found that he could earn money by singing at weddings.

Again he only earned a few kronen but through the combination of painting and singing he was able to support himself.

This new found independence had a profound effect upon him. Confidence in himself grew and for the first time in his life he began to feel happy. He made time to go for walks along the coast and through the forest in order to paint landscapes.

The life of most artists is a precarious one whether they paint postcards or portraits, and at a time when Elof had few buyers for his work he decided to use his small savings to go into business – a street sausage stand. He found a site, bought a cart and a sausage boiler and arranged for a young assistant who would actually take the hot sausages from the boiler and serve them while Elof supervised and performed the necessary public relations by chatting amiably to the customers.

All that was now required was a license from the authorities which, to Elof's shocked amazement was turned down. He was informed of a regulation stating that a licence could only be granted to the owner of a sausage stand if he actually lifted the sausages from the boiler himself which in Elof's case was impossible.

While doing his best to accept this disappointment Elof's luck had changed. Erich Stegmann, who had been searching for disabled artists for his projected co-operative, heard of the mouth-painter in Stockholm who eked out a living by selling postcards he drew. He saw Elof's work, arranged for him to have private tuition and then, in July 1956, invited him to become a member of the fledgling partnership.

The next year Elof travelled to Vaduz to attend the Association's first general meeting. This was the watershed in his life. From then on he was not only financially independent but was recognised for what he really was – a talented professional artist. Instead of his original cards being sold in cafes, reproductions of them brought pleasure to people all over the world, and he continued to win great critical acclaim for his paintings until his death in 1986.

Another original member of the Association whose work was an important factor in its establishment was Carl Fischer. He was a professional artist in Germany before the Second World War and after it broke out he was called up for military service and sent to Prague. In 1944 he was due for leave and he sent a telegram to his wife in Amorbach, 'The day after tomorrow I will be with you. Love, Carl.'

The train which was taking him home had just pulled into the station at Fulda when an air raid warning sounded. Passengers leapt from the carriages and raced towards the air raid shelter outside the station as the first bombs began to explode. Carl threw himself to the ground and instinctively raised his hands to protect his head. A bomb burst close by and one of its splinters amputated both his arms.

When the news reached his wife she had only one thought and that was to be at his side. Travel at that stage of the war was almost impossible for civilians but nothing could deter her. She walked, hitched rides on trucks and somehow managed to get aboard a troop train only to be put off whenever the military police spotted her – and pulled on board again by the soldiers when the MPs had gone. After three days she reached the hospital where her husband lay racked both by physical agony and agony of mind – if he survived what future could there be for an artist without arms?

After three weeks, during which his wife never left his bedside, Carl's despair lifted. If his wife was so happy that he was still alive even though maimed, he should rejoice that he had such loving support. And with his change of mood the doctors announced that his injuries were healing faster than they thought possible.

One morning his wife said to him, 'Carl, do you remember that holiday we had before the war in Mittenwald and the man we saw painting in the market square?'

'You mean the crippled one who held the brush in his mouth?'

'Yes. He seemed so full of life when he talked to us, and he managed to paint so well ...'

'All right,' said Carl. 'I will give this mouth-painting a month's trial.'

Well aware that his future depended on mastering this new technique he drove himself desperately to regain his old skill. When he was finally satisfied that he had done so he returned to the office of the West German magazine for which he used to work and here he introduced a new pictorial character known as Tom Cat Oscar who was always attired in distinctive black trousers, red-striped jumper and a blue tie. The comic adventures and domestic tribulations of Tom Cat Oscar, modelled by Carl's pet white and ginger cat, proved immensely popular not only in the magazine but in several books which sold over a million copies.

One day in Vaduz Carl Fischer had a meeting with the disabled artist he had watched years earlier in Mittenwald – Erich Stegmann. And as a result he became one of the Association's first members.

Another professional artist invited by Erich Stegmann to join his fledgling organisation was Pieter Moleveld, the son of a Dutch architect, who was completing his art studies when Holland was invaded at the onset of the Second World War. Food soon became in short supply but the Moleveld family sometimes had extra because Pieter was asked by grocers to design food advertisements to put in their windows in lieu of the real thing. He was adamant that he could not paint cheeses, hams, baskets of eggs and so on unless he had models to work from, and as some of his commissions came from the royal victuallers he was suitably supplied.

The family also eked out their rations by growing huge quantities of French beans. When the crop was ready it was traditional for friends to take part in the picking and preserving, a task largely done by women because towards the end of the war most men had been drafted to work in Germany. Pieter was about to go to an optics factory when bean-picking time came around. Among those present for the harvest was a family friend with her daughter Margarethe who worked alongside Pieter. The two young people had a happy day together, and in the evening when he saw her home he asked her if she would model for him.

'I was afraid at the time that it would be immoral,' Margarethe admitted much later. In reality it was not immoral but hard work as Pieter painted her over and over again until he plucked up enough courage to propose. After that they celebrated each anniversary of their wedding with a meal in which French beans were the main ingredient.

When peace returned to Europe Pieter became well-known as a painter at the Haager School. He and Margarethe had three children and when their eldest was ten years old they planned to get a larger apartment in which Pieter would have a more spacious studio.

These plans were dashed in September 1956 when Pieter was suddenly taken ill and within hours poliomyelitis was diagnosed. In the hospital Margarethe had to give her consent for a tracheal operation to be performed in order for him to breathe by means of artificial respiration. Thanks to this surgery he survived but was left with his limbs paralysed and his mind darkened by depression – he felt his career as an artist was over and with it his means of supporting his family.

After a year in which he found it very difficult to adjust to his new condition, it was suggested that, as he still had a little movement in his foot, he might try painting with a brush held in his toes. He was reluctant to try until his old teacher Pieter van Boreel encouraged him. At first Pieter was ever more depressed because he found it impossible to manipulate the brush and he protested that he felt like a three-year-old trying to paint.

Pieter van Boreel made him persevere and finally he succeeded in producing a foot painting which was as good as the paintings he had done in the days when he enjoyed good health. Now he could only breathe normally for two hours a day, the rest of the time he had to rely on oxygen which he received from hospital-supplied cylinders through a respiratory device implanted near his larynx.

It was impossible for him to return to the Haager School but after Erich Stegmann had asked him to paint for the Association he was able to earn his living at home, his pictures of evocative Dutch landscapes setting a standard of excellence for the cards produced by the new organisation.

Many other painters who came after Elof Lundberg, Carl Fischer and Pieter Moleveld have contributed greatly to the growth of the Association of Mouth and Foot Painting Artists but no retrospective chapter would be complete without mention of Peter Spencer MBE who did so much to further the organisation.

He achieved much as an artist and a great deal outside the world of art, and if he owed a lot to the Association the Association came to owe a lot to him. Yet in the beginning, unlike the other artists described in this book, he was not regarded as talented enough to be taken on as a student. After sending in some of his paintings he received the following reply: 'Thank you for sending us samples of your work but we regret that your paintings do not come up to the standard we require for publication.'

Peter Spencer was fifteen and a pupil of Oldershaw Grammar School in Wallasey in what is now designated Merseyside at the outbreak of the Second World War. When the Air Training Corps was formed in Wallasey he enthusiastically joined 273 Squadron. Later he enlisted in the RAF and in the summer of 1943 he sailed out of Liverpool bound for the No 5 British Flying Training School at Clewiston in Florida.

After wartime Britain America was a revelation to the young airmen; no blackout, no shortage of food and a dizzy social life as hospitable Americans wanted to entertain the boys who were going to fly against Hitler. But, as Peter told the author some time ago, there was a dark side to the sunshine life. The cadets were warned that two of their number had been killed on each course.

'It was an uncomfortable feeling to think that two of us might not make it – that it might be me in a training crash,' he said. 'And sure enough two of our chaps did get killed. Altogether over thirty RAF cadets died during training at Clewiston, and there is a special cemetery for them where there is a ceremony of remembrance held every year.'

Peter won his 'Wings' in February 1944 and returned to Britain to fly Dakotas of Transport Command. He began operational flying in September with 512 Squadron of 46 Group Transport Command at Broadwell in Oxfordshire. He and his crew of three flew their Dakotas on regular runs across the Channel to carry supplies to the forward units in the invasion of France. In February of the following year he was promoted to Flight Sergeant and soon he was flying to the Rhine in support of the crossing there, returning with his aircraft scarred by anti-aircraft flak.

On 27 March Peter had a rest day but an urgent job came up and he volunteered to fly four officers to Rheims in an Anson aircraft. As the truck took them out to their plane on the tarmac a taxi-ing Mosquito bomber caught the vehicle with its starboard propeller and Peter's right arm was shorn off.

When he came round in hospital he realized that not only had he lost one arm but the other was paralysed. The first thought that came into his head was 'I'll never play the piano again.' The pain was indescribable and could only be held at bay with injections of morphine.

In order to rehabilitate him when he came out of hospital the Air Ministry department dealing with the resettlement of airmen arranged for him to go to the Central School of Speech Training and Dramatic Art in London in order for him to try for a job with the BBC as an announcer. It was an imaginative idea but one thing had been overlooked until the audition – in his condition it was impossible for him to handle the pages of a script or flick the necessary switches.

Returning to his parents' home in Wallasey Peter, now twenty-four and on a hundred percent war disability pension of £2 4s 0d. a week, began giving elocution lessons. Then, in July 1950, he met the girl he was destined to marry. One day he went for a walk to the New Brighton pier where a show called 'Happy Time' was being performed in the open-air theatre, and as he approached it he saw a girl on the stage singing 'O My Beloved Father'. Her looks and vitality had a great impact on Peter while June Lynette, when she left the stage, carried the mental picture of a handsome young man with dark curling hair who had not taken his eyes off her during the performance. And she was not at all surprised that he was waiting for her after the show.

It was only then that she realized that the right sleeve of his jacket was empty. Peter explained simply that he had not only lost one arm but also the use of the other. June's reaction could not have been better – she merely said, 'How interesting.' And agreed to meet him that evening.

In the bar of the Grand Hotel June raised his glass to his lips for him as though she had known him for ages – indeed, in a curious way she felt she had – and so their romance began.

What worried Peter was the thought that if she agreed to marry him, how could he provide for her, and perhaps a family, on a disability pension supplemented by what he could earn teaching elocution? When he finally raised this she brushed it aside.

'I was sent to marry and look after you,' she said. 'I have always known that.'

They married on 12 December 1951 in St Nicholas's Church in Wallasey.

It was through one of Ripley's *Belive It or Not* cartoon features that Peter first learned of Erich Stegmann, a disabled German artist who painted by holding a brush in his mouth. The story fascinated Peter and he tried the technique. It was far more difficult than he had expected but he was filled with an ambition to emulate Stegmann. Towards Christmas he came across some cards published by the Association of Mouth and Foot Painting Artists and, thinking he might be on the brink of a new career, he sent off six paintings and waited eagerly for the verdict. When it came it was to turn him down.

While the Association did not feel his standard was high enough, he was not forgotten and some months later he was invited to an exhibition of members' work. And there he came face-to-face with the man who he had learned about through Ripley – Erich Stegmann. Through an interpreter the founder of the Association repeated that while Peter's work showed talent it was not sufficiently developed, and then added, 'I suggest that you attend an art school and we will give you a scholarship to cover the cost of your tuition and materials.'

Peter took a course at the Wallasey School of Art. His determination to make painting a career was given a new impetus when his son Robin was born in 1958 – their second child Jill Rosemary arrived in 1962 – and next year any doubts he had about providing for his family ended when at an Association conference in Edinburgh it was announced that he had been given full membership.

Apart from the financial benefits which came with membership, it strengthened Peter's confidence in other directions. In 1960 he stood for the local council, won the Marlowe Ward and held it with an ever-increasing majority for the next fourteen years; he served as Chairman of the Wallasey Arts Society and President and Chairman of the Merseyside Branch of the British Limbless Ex-Servicemen's Association. Finding that he could speak well and amusingly in public he took on the job of public relations officer for the Association which entailed travelling overseas to promote the work of his fellow artists.

In 1970 Peter's biography *No Man An Island* by Eileen Waugh, with a foreword by Douglas Bader, became a best seller and when it was translated into French the Humanitarian society *Merite et Devouement Francais* awarded him *Le Croix de Commandeur* for 'exceptional services to humanity' through the example he gave to others in adversity.

Peter's best moment came in 1980 when he went to Buckingham Palace to be invested with the MBE. As Her Majesty realized that she could not shake hands with him she placed her hand on his left sleeve before pinning the award on his lapel.

Two years later Peter became a Deputy Lieutenant of the County of Merseyside and because many of his paintings reflected his early love of flying, the Guild of Aviation Artists elected him as Associate Member. Yet no matter how busy Peter was he continued painting right up to his death in 1987 and he never tired of working enthusiastically to further the cause of the Association.

Writing of Peter's painting, the art historian Dr Richard Hiepe said, 'His passion for flying, from which he was barred by his accident is expressed in his magically overdrawn "portraits" of the giant aeroplanes of the jet age. They are not photographic descriptions, but homages to a novel kind of beauty.'

Without doubt Elizabeth Twistington Higgins was the best known of Britain's mouth painters – and the most handicapped. Her story has been told on the *This Is Your Life* programme and in books, including her own *Still Life* and the biography *The Dance Goes On*. An hour-long film of the same name has been shown several times on

British television and on many television channels around the world. Named the Best Documentary of 1980 by the magazine *Films and Filming*, it endeavoured to tell the story of Elizabeth's past life and show her at work not only at her specially designed easel but also putting her remarkable ballet group the Chelmsford Dancers through their graceful paces.

Narrated by Rudolf Nureyev, the film used still photographs to tell the story of Elizabeth's early life. When the Second World War began the Twistington Higgins family returned from holiday to their home in Highgate, London, to find that the only school left open was a dancing academy. Elizabeth, Brighid and Alison, the three daughters of Thomas Twistington Higgins, a celebrated pioneer of children's surgery, were enrolled and enjoyed two hours of dancing practice before ordinary lessons every morning.

For Elizabeth the new regime was a delight as she had dreamed of a career as a ballet dancer ever since the age of fourteen after being taken to Sadler's Wells for a magical performance of Les Sylphides by her brother. Later when she mentioned her ambition to her father he replied with the infuriating logic of adults that she must finish her normal education before considering such an insecure career. But when she matriculated he agreed that she could apply for training at Sadler's Wells.

After a short try-out period Elizabeth's high hopes were dashed when she was told from a physical point of view she was not suited for the Sadler's Wells company. If her hopes were dashed they were not extinguished, and she went to a school run by the famous Cone Sisters – known today as The Arts Educational School – where she earned her Advanced Ballet certificate and won the prestigious Solo Seal in 1945 after which she became a teacher at the school.

Elizabeth enjoyed teaching and later became known as the Penny Ballerina when she taught pre-school children at Coram Fields, the well-known playground in Bloomsbury, and organized 'penny concerts' at which musicians from the Royal Academy of Music gave up Saturday mornings to perform for the local children.

Meanwhile she auditioned for and was accepted as a member of the musical *Song of Norway* at the Palace Theatre in Shaftesbury Avenue which ran for fourteen months, after which she did film and television work, and took part in a pantomime at the London Palladium. Next she successfully auditioned for Ivor Novello's *King's Rhapsody* in which she danced until the musical closed several months after the death of Novello in 1951.

By now Elizabeth found that teaching gave her more satisfaction than performing, and she started her own classes at the Art Workers' Guild Hall in London's Queen Square, opposite the National Hospital for Nervous Diseases. During the 1953 poliomyelitis epidemic it was to this hospital that Elizabeth was rushed by ambulance after she had been taken ill at her parents' home in Mongeham, Kent. Here polio was diagnosed and in Elizabeth's words 'they whizzed me out of the ward, wheeled me along seemingly endless corridors to a room on Ward 12 where I was shoved in an iron lung, and that was that!'

When the film on Elizabeth's life came to be made the problem was how to portray the onset of the illness that completely paralysed her apart from a very slight movement in her right hand. The idea of using an actress to play Elizabeth's part was discarded, instead it was decided to recreate the episode by showing an ambulance racing into Queen Square, the hospital staff taking the stretcher inside and ending at the iron lung. The camera was to be mounted on the stretcher so that the viewers would see everything as Elizabeth saw it that long-ago day and have the sensation of being slid into the coffin-like breathing machine.

And here the film team experienced one of the many remarkable coincidences that occurred during the making of *The Dance Goes On*. Over a quarter of a century had passed since Elizabeth had been driven to the National Hospital – where did one get an ambulance of the 'fifties from?

It was found that there is an Ambulance Museum and it could provide a suitable vehicle with driver. After the ambulance and arrival had been filmed in Queen Square, the driver remarked that out of all the ambulances that had been on the road in 1953 this was the actual one that had brought Elizabeth up from Kent.

When asked how he could be sure, he replied that the driver of the ambulance had joined the staff of the Ambulance Museum and had passed on the anecdote – he would have driven the vehicle himself only he happened to be retiring that very day.

Iron lungs, too, had changed and the helpful authorities at the National Hospital tried to discover if there was an old model still in existence. They located one at the Royal National Orthopaedic Hospital in Stanmore and when the film crew arrived there they were told that this surviving lung had originally come from the National Hospital and would have been the one used by Elizabeth. As more coincidences followed the crew began to expect a new one every day, even such minor examples as a hire-car driver remarking out of the blue that he had lived next door to the Twistington Higgins family as a child.

In the National Hospital for Nervous Diseases Elizabeth remained very ill for a long time, dependent for life on the iron lung whose varying pressure kept her lungs working. The children she taught lit candles for her in the local Roman Catholic church and Margot Fonteyn, whose marriage took place at this time, sent her bridal bouquet – one of the many tokens of love that Elizabeth received from her friends in the ballet world.

Physiotherapists tried to restore Elizabeth's neck muscles so that she could use them to consciously draw air into her lungs and twenty-seven months after she had been stricken she was able to remain outside the lung for up to four hours. Her every breath was performed by a deliberate mental command to the accessory breathing muscles in her neck – a process known as 'frog' breathing – and these commands had to be given consciously no matter what else she had to think about. She once described the process to the author as like having two tunes running through her head simultaneously. And because breathing was a conscious effort for Elizabeth she had to sleep in an iron lung each night.

A great moment in her life came when she left the hospital for her first brief outing in Queen Square. Taken from the lung, she was laid on a trolley from the operating theatre and escorted by two nurses, a physiotherapist and a doctor, she was wheeled round the square while from every window of the hospital waving hands showed that both patients and staff shared her triumph.

From the National Hospital Elizabeth went to the Royal National Orthopaedic Hospital in Stanmore; later she was able to stay with her parents thanks to a portable cuirass-type respirator and the help of a visiting physiotherapist and district nurse. But a severe winter ended this for fear that storm would bring down the electricity cables and her respirator would go dead. On several occasions this happened and her parents had to hurriedly take her out of her lung so that she could begin 'frog' breathing. These alarming incidents made her realize that her being at home was becoming too difficult for her mother and father and regretfully she planned to become hospitalized again.

In 1957 she was moved from her home to the British Polio Fellowship Hostel. Here there were no staff members on duty during the afternoons which Elizabeth found frustrating because there was no one to turn the pages of her book. Other patients managed this with mouthsticks, and Elizabeth wondered whether it would be possible for her to hold one in her teeth and breathe at the same time. After a lot of effort Elizabeth mastered the stick without it affecting her breathing and the turning of a page became the first thing she was able to do for herself for four years.

The mouthstick was the precursor of the mouth-held paintbrush. One of the Friends of the Hostel named Rosie suggested Elizabeth might pass some of the time by painting and, despite her first almost hilarious attempts when the paint splattered everywhere, Elizabeth found it fun. Like some other severely disabled people whose condition makes them difficult to be categorized, Elizabeth was then transferred again, this time to the Dover Isolation Hospital, and here a breakthrough in her painting came when she took regular lessons with a local art teacher named Rosemary Howard.

'It took Elizabeth nine months to master the technique of loading her brush with paint,' Rosemary told the author. 'She could not move her head forward very far so the board had to be moved into the orbit of her brush. Sometimes she would do a pleasing sketch and then, quite unexpectedly, jerk. The brush would slither down and all that effort would be wasted.'

As Elizabeth's skill progressed and she began to paint her famous ballet pictures. Rosemary commented later, 'Obviously, inside herself she was dancing with those figures. When they were poised on one foot I felt she was somehow part of them; it was her arms that were extended, and she was on the stage under the lights.'

Elizabeth's father used a reproduction of one of her paintings for a Christmas card in 1958 and this led to her being interviewed by a journalist from a London paper, and his story in turn led to Elizabeth's first exhibition held at the Dover School of Art.

Word of Elizabeth's talent spread and in 1961 fifty of her paintings were used in coloured panels in the Queen's reception room during the Festival of Ballet's Christmas season at the Royal Festival Hall. The following year she appeared on *This Is Your Life*. After the programme there was such a demand for her pictures that soon she had none left to sell, and with this success came the dream of leading an independent life again. It was a dream that became a reality after she was asked to join the Association of Mouth and Foot Painting Artist.

The film of *The Dance Goes On* was able to demonstrate what independence meant to Elizabeth by showing a day in her life, starting at the Broomfield Hospital in Chelmsford where she had to spend every night in an iron lung. Once she had been prepared for the day Elizabeth was taken by her own ambulance to her house. A rota of helpers ensured that she was properly cared for while on her wheelchair was mounted a POSM – Patient Operated Selector Mechanism. By blowing into a plastic mouthpiece Elizabeth was able to activate the device to summon her helper, control the temperature and lighting and make calls on the telephone.

Because Elizabeth's neck movement was so restricted and therefore did not allow her much range on her canvas when painting, a special motorized easel was made for her by Doug Adams, an engineer whose hobby is designing equipment for the disabled. Apart from her neck muscles Elizabeth's only movement was in a finger in her right hand. At the slightest pressure on micro switches set in a plastic cast the easel's board moved up and down and sideways.

Apart from her art work Elizabeth wrote a book on her experiences entitled *Still Life* which was published in 1969. For this she used an electric typewriter which she also operated with her right hand positioned over the keyboard in a special sling attached to an overhead support.

But the most remarkable of her achievements was her return to ballet teaching. Soon after Elizabeth had settled into the routine of her new home Joan Weston, the honorary director and founder of the Chelmsford Ballet Company, asked if she would be interested in producing a tarantella for eight girls in a forthcoming production. Despite misgivings Elizabeth accepted the challenge.

'I shall never forget how I met Elizabeth,' recalls one of the Chelmsford Ballet dancers involved. 'I was there for some casting auditions and she was coming to see the dancers and choose those she wanted. At that time I knew nothing about her, except that she was a lady in a wheelchair and everybody spoke with great reverence and in hushed voices. "Oh, that's Miss Twistington Higgins coming ..." And there she was. All the doors were opened wide and some of us helped to lift her wheelchair up three steps into the studio. Everyone stood around in awed silence. All the girls stopped chattering, and this very frail, thin person started to address us ..."

The tarantella was a great success and followed in 1971 with Elizabeth arranging dance sequences for an experimental Eucharist in Chelmsford Cathedral. The performance was so moving that many members of the congregation were in tears – and Elizabeth knew that she wanted to continue with liturgical ballet.

To this end she formed her own ballet company, the Chelmsford Dancers, who for the next eleven years performed all over the country in cathedrals, churches, hospitals and even in prisons. Helped by her assistant director Sheila Large, Elizabeth managed to do everything, from the choreography to designing the costumes with her mouth-held brush. A practice session of Elizabeth's dancers was filmed, with Elizabeth using a POSM-operated tape recorder to provide the music, and then the camera was taken to All Souls in Langham Place, London, where a glorious performance was recorded.

Ballet work did not replace Elizabeth's art work for the Association of Mouth and Foot Painting Artists, and in 1977 she was taken to Buckingham Palace to receive from Her Majesty the Queen the order of the MBE in recognition of her skill as a painter.

Elizabeth described the moment when she was wheeled forward and the Queen stepped down from her dais and placed the order on the little hook which had been attached to her blouse for the purpose thus, 'Her Majesty is very petite, being little higher than I was sitting in my wheelchair. Her voice was soft and melodious, and she seemed to generate kindliness. And how well she must have done her homework. That morning nearly two hundred people came before her and only the name of the recipient was announced with no hint as to what they were being honoured for. Yet Her Majesty had words for everybody, and when it was my turn she had a long talk to me about my painting. Then, by way of dismissal, she said, "I do hope this outing has not tired you too much." The page took control of the wheelchair and I was rolled away a Member of the British Empire.'

Four years after the film on Elizabeth's life was shown on television several of the Chelmsford Dancers could no longer continue due to domestic and career reasons and Elizabeth, rather than let the company's standards drop, decided it was best 'to go out on a high'.

Elizabeth died suddenly and without pain in September 1990 at her home in Chelmsford. When working on the film of her life the author asked her what she regarded as her ultimate goal to which she answered, 'I should think a nice little dance in Heaven.' If anyone deserved such a modest reward it is Elizabeth and no doubt for her the dance goes on.

John Bunce

'I was bored out of my mind'

A person's life can be altered in a single second so that for however many more years he, or she, may live nothing will ever be the same again. So it was for twenty-year-old John Bunce when in 1952 he was doing his National Service in the British Army's catering corps in Germany, work he enjoyed so much he had resolved to train to be a chef when he was demobbed.

One evening in his billet after coming off duty, he stood by his bed and reached up to replace a book on a high shelf and he somehow missed his footing. As he felt himself fall he twisted so that he would land on his bed, and as he did so a blinding pain shot through his head. What he had not known was that a metal toolbox had been pushed under the bed. That was what his head had struck.

Lying as he had fallen he found it impossible to move and that he could speak no louder than a whisper. An inconsequential thought flashed through his brain: 'Now I shall get out of the C.O.'s inspection tomorrow.'

His second thought was that it might be 'the end of the line', as he put it. As a boy he had sung in a church choir, and now thought of the faith he had been taught returned to him. In his almost inaudible voice he asked his fellow soldiers who stood shocked around the bed to repeat the Lord's Prayer with him.

'It was remarkable how much it helped me at that moment,' recalls John who for the last few years has been a member of the Christadelphian Church.

When John arrived in a military hospital he could not speak at all, and it was found that he had broken his fifth vertebra with the result that he was paralysed from the neck down. From Germany he was taken to the Stoke Mandeville Hospital's special injury unit where he was subjected to intensive physiotherapy. His doctors were particularly interested in him because at the time he had the highest lesion of the vertebra they had seen.

With treatment John's voice returned and also enough movement in one arm to be able to pilot an electric wheelchair by means of a special 'joystick', but after two years it was realized there could be no further improvement and the young man was sent home to his parents.

While at the hospital John remembers he was 'bored out of his mind' and that he could not sit like some of the others making 'baskets and fluffy dolls'. In order to occupy him with something that was not beyond his very limited capability a member of staff suggested he might like to try 'painting by numbers' by means of a brush held in his mouth.

The first attempt was not inspiring but looking back on it John thinks that everything started from there.

Then, when John went home to his parents, the idea of occupying himself by means of a pencil in his mouth presented itself again.

'To pass the time while I lay in bed I used to read those little comic war books, and with a pencil I copied some of the pictures – a face or a tank – in the margin,' he recalls. 'I really enjoyed this, especially when my mother was out and I was left alone in the house and had to fill the time as best I could.'

From the margins of comics John progressed to sketching on scrap paper, much to the surprise of a welfare official who urged John to enter a pencil sketch in an art competition.

When it was announced that John Bunce was the winner it gave him the encouragement he needed to take this art further, especially as the judges had had no idea that the man responsible for the winning entry was disabled. At that time John's problem with his work was that for some reason he was nervous of colour and when he made his first attempt with water-colours his worst fears were confirmed. Propped up in bed, he found that the paint ran down the paper quicker than he could control it with his brush, and soon the coverlet was damp and tinted with pale colours. Yet when the brushes were put away and paintbox closed John knew that he wanted to try again.

Soon the painting became John's only escape from the grimmer realities of life.

'I had split up with my wife – she had found someone else as so often happens when a husband or wife becomes disabled,' he says. 'And while I was back in hospital for a spell I learned that my father was suffering from cancer. What I wanted most was to be close to where my Dad was. The only way I could do this was to go into a Cheshire Home in Wolverhampton which being only eight miles away enabled me to visit him frequently.'

At one time or another several members of the Mouth and Foot Painting Artists Association have stayed in Cheshire Homes which were the inspiration of Group Captain Leonard Cheshire VC OM, who got the idea of founding such an establishment after he had taken a serviceman who was dying of cancer into his own home. His aim was to make them as 'un-institutional' as possible, to be places of shelter and spiritual encouragement. The first of these homes was Le Court in Hampshire where the well-known mouth artist Albert Baker lived for a long time. Today there are many Cheshire Homes in Britain and abroad and they are open for any disabled person to apply for residence without any reference to race or religion.

'I would recommend this type of establishment to anyone with a serious disability,' says John. 'It doesn't restrict you. You are not a prisoner within your own four walls. Of course it is lovely to be at home, it's private and you have your relatives round you, but it doesn't give you very much scope. At a Cheshire Home, whether you are trying to do artwork or writing or whatever, you get a fair amount of criticism and encouragement from the staff and visitors.'

In fact John found that Le Court suited him so well that he stayed there for seven years and then transferred to the Greenacres Cheshire Home in Sutton Coldfield where he lives today.

Meanwhile his interest in drawing and painting persisted and in 1974 it was suggested that he should contact the Association of Mouth and Foot Painting Artists, an organisation he had never heard of until then. After some of his paintings were evaluated he became a student and then a member eleven years later. The period of learning was very useful to John who, he admits, had never been taught anything about art. He says the most important thing he learned was to be critical of his own work to the point when he would scrap a painting if he felt it did not come up to standard.

John's work has won him a number of prizes. Recently he achieved the highest award in the DHSS national art competition and also claimed the top awards for water-colours and oils in the independent regional competition. In these competitions paintings are considered without the judges knowning the names of the artists responsible for them.

Health permitting, John works every day in a room at Greenacres whose glass walls overlook a garden and which makes a perfect studio. He works at an easel which he designed himself. Electric motors tilt the board and raise it up and down but what is so special about it is that John can control it with a mouthstick which has a magnet mounted on the end. A touch of the magnet on one of the squares set in a panel is enough to activate the mechanism.

Another of his innovations is a light metal frame which clamps on to the arms of his wheelchair and holds his camera at eye level. Photography is useful to him when he wants to capture a scene for future painting when out in the countryside and composition is achieved by manoeuvring his electric wheelchair.

John is catholic in his choice of subjects and the materials he uses which include coloured inks, oils and water-colours.

'I enjoy painting whatever I am painting at the time,' he says. 'I have no preference at all. I like painting a woodland scene as much as a house, a seascape as much as a bowl of flowers.'

An intriguing aspect of John's work is his secret 'signature'; in every picture he incorporates a minute rabbit which may be no more than a shape caused by shadow or a rabbit-shaped patch of sky seen through foliage. Children who come to watch him work regard his pictures as puzzles as they seek the hidden bunny.

Apart from giving art lessons to both children and adults John does a lot of work for charitable causes through demonstrations of his mouth-painting technique at church fêtes and similar gatherings, and he is also invited to schools.

He says, 'Usually I go for a whole morning or afternoon but sometimes when it is a large school I go for a whole day. To win the pupil's interest I do an on-the-spot portrait of whoever has a birthday that day, or whose birthday is closest. I tell them about being disabled and about my work so that I try to get across to them that if a person is in a wheelchair he or she is approachable.

'Like everyone I do have some regrets, one being that I did not meet Erich Stegmann who founded the Association and did so much to help people like me. Although you can work on your own as a disabled artist, the Association gives you something to aim for and it enables you to meet other artists who are in your situation.'

Florence Bunn

A Love Story

'You will not find this a story of triumph in the face of adversity,' Florence Bunn told the author. 'It is a love story.' And as she continued it became obvious what she meant.

Memories of her young days are very happy ones. Her father was an artistic craftsman of many talents, one of which was sign-writing the names of firms on glass doors in gold leaf. He was so proficient that he could put the lettering on backwards as was required without the help of a mirror which was the usual method employed. Florence remembers what a treat it was to be allowed to watch him, holding back any coughs or sneezes because gold leaf is so light the slightest movement of the air could carry it away.

Florence, who had been born in West Hartlepool in 1937, enjoyed being a schoolgirl and this fostered the ambition to become a teacher. To this end she later went to St. Hilda's College in Durham where she specialized in mathematics. In 1955 this was still regarded as an unusual subject for a woman to undertake and she had to attend a male college for lectures.

When she had completed her course Florence returned home to teach in a girl's secondary school which was amalgamated with a boys' school in the early 'sixties.

'I stayed at the school for nine years,' Florence says. 'I found time to be a youth leader three nights a week and I became involved in the Church Young Fellowship as well. I was a lucky young woman enjoying amateur dramatics, playing tennis and badminton – occasionally with the man who was to become my husband. Who says that game-love means you've lost!'

This man was Geoff Bunn and he had known Florence from their babyhood.

'Our parents who lived in the same street were friends before we were born,' explains Geoff. 'And we were born within weeks of each other. We still have a photograph of us both taken at the age of eighteen months. Our families went on holiday together and if the war had not come along they would have emigrated to Canada together. Today I still find it strange that Florence can tell me anecdotes about my relatives that I have never heard before.

'During the war my father moved the family to Blackpool – he still had memories of West Hartlepool being bombarded in the first World War when he was a young apprentice – but we used to go back for holidays and my highlight of the week was to sit on the same settee as Florence, eating fish and chips and then singing songs round the piano – as we still do.'

This way Geoff and Florence remained in contact until she went to college and he served in the navy when they lost touch for eight years.

'In 1965 a cousin of mine invited me to a wedding in Hartlepool,' says Geoff. 'I went and found that Florence was there. This time there was no question of us losing contact.'

It was about this time that Florence found that minor things were going wrong with her health. Once her tongue became numb and fingers tingled strangely but after a few days these odd symptoms disappeared. Her doctor told her that as the educational system was going through massive changes at the time she was finding it stressful and all she needed was a few days' rest.

'I was young and enthusiastic and I just thought my body was warning me to slow down a bit,' says Florence. 'in July 1966 Geoff and I were married. I continued teaching for another couple of years until my first son was born. Our second son was born in 1971 and I had a hint that all was not well during the pregnancy. Soon afterwards multiple sclerosis was diagnosed.

'One of the unfortunate spin-offs of early MS is that one looks drunk because of the loss of balance and whereas a helpful hand would be nice the reality is a cold shoulder. I began to use elbow crutches but I found housework and looking after two active toddlers becoming more and more difficult so I went back to education as a home tutor and was able to pay for help in the house.

'Home tutors are a band of people who take on the education of youngsters who usually – through illness – have been away from school and need special help to catch up. I found I had to teach everything and they were four happy years because I really felt I was doing something worthwhile. One of my early pupils was a girl with a spinal problem and I was so pleased when the other day she brought round her daughter to meet me.

'At home we began using labour-saving gadgets that were almost ahead of my time. A washing-machine, dishwasher, foodmixer and so on eased the problems of two small boys and my husband who still prefers homecooking.'

By 1977 a new gadget had to be introduced – an electric wheelchair but due to the inexorable progress of the disease Florence began to lose the use of her hands with the result that she was unable to control the chair. One day the postman brought her green employment card from the Education Office.

"Dear Geoff didn't tell me about it at first and when I did find out it was a psychological blow – I was unemployable,' Florence recalls. 'I started going out to a day care centre one day a week and was very unhappy for a very long time. It was nobody's fault but I could not get used to the idea of being disabled, of not even being able to feed myself.

'Eventually a young instructor anxious to find something that would fill in my time suggested drawing by mouth. I remember how hard he searched the building for a suitable table and pencil-holder for me to use. I felt silly but he had tried so hard the least I could do was try as well.'

As Florence became proficient in using mouth-held pencils and brushes she wondered how she could put her new-found interest into practical use. In 1983 she hit on the idea of designing decorative stationery and having it printed to sell at a craft fair. Soon afterwards she received a letter from the Association of Mouth and Foot Painting Artists asking her if she would send in some examples of her work. Apparently a reporter covering the fair had described the stationery produced by Florence – the headline read 'The Art of Florence' – and a cutting of the story reached the Association in London.

When there was no immediate response Florence sent in more of her work to prove that her first consignment was not 'a flash in the pan'. Soon afterwards she was offered a studentship.

'An immediate benefit was that I began to believe more in myself,' Florence says. 'We think we don't constantly want admiration yet underneath we do. What I mean is that we want to be accepted, we want someone to notice us. And the important thing about becoming a student is that you have someone backing you. And what I did not realize was how many fellow mouth and foot painting students there are in the world.

'It was like joining a great big family that you kept in touch with through our international magazine. And then there were the exhibitions of members' work. I remember going down to London to a big exhibition in the Royal Festival Hall and seeing the paintings there I realized how much harder I needed to work and they inspired me because they showed me just what could be done. Then – and at the other exhibitions I have been invited to since – I come away saying to myself, "If I try harder I might just manage that."'

'When we got back to our home in Blackpool Geoff built me an easel with a board powered by a little electric motor so that it moves up and down and gives me much more scope. I also had to find a better way of moving in front of the easel. I had begun sitting in an armchair but I could not move back to see what I had done.' This problem was finally solved by a specially adapted electric wheelchair which she can control by movement of her chin on a suitably shaped control bar.

Florence worked on with a determination to become a full member. At first she had produced postcard-sized pictures but the motorized easel Geoff had made increased her scope. She tried, and still uses, several media for the separate challenge each one provides. Her favourite subject was – and still is – still life studies of flowers which Geoff picks for her in the garden of their home.

Able-bodied artists will agree that painting is not an easy occupation. It requires continual concentration both mental and physical and the need to remain more or less in one position in front of an easel for long periods. How much more problematic for a disabled person like Florence with the added difficulty of only having movement from the base of her neck up and being in frequent pain.

'Because I want to remain clear-headed through the day for the sake of my family as well as for the sake of my work I do not take any pain-killers though at night I do have to take something to make me sleep,' she explains. 'Painting takes my mind off the discomfort. It's the best pain-killer I know and there are no side effects.'

Florence's hard work paid off. She became a full member of the Association in March 1988.

Thanks to the financial security this meant Geoff was able to give up his job with British Telecom in order to look after Florence full-time though she still jealously guards what little independence is left to her.

'I like to paint by myself as much as possible,' she says. 'Of course Geoff has to put the paints out for me but when that is done I am left alone to get on with it. I could not feel I was doing it by myself if someone was helping me too much.'

Apart from her paintings which are sent to the Association Florence likes to experiment in other fields. She paints on porcelain which Geoff fires for her in her own kiln. Some of the vases she showed the author were quite remarkable with abstract decoration composed of spattered paint and gilded.

'To get the effect I mixed the paint with milk and blew it on with a straw,' she laughed. 'The gold I put on with a brush. I like that part – perhaps it reminds me of watching my father work with gold. With ceramics there is the thought that unless they get broken my work is there forever.'

Another aspect of becoming a full member of the Association which delighted Florence was that it gave her the sense of belonging to a world-wide family. After it was announced in the Association's journal that she had been accepted as a member she received a letter from India written by a disabled artist there who had become a member on the same day and an interesting amusing correspondence has continued ever since. A similar letter arrived from Canada and there are opportunities for her to meet her fellow painters on the occasions when conferences are arranged.

'It has given life a whole new meaning,' she says, 'though I sometimes have the artist's equivalent to writer's block. A blank piece of water-colour paper can be quite daunting, intimidating almost. One answer for me is to change completely my medium for a short time, and paint small intricate designs on china.'

After firing, these items form the nucleus of a small one-woman exhibition which is set up whenever she gives a talk about the MFPA, thus encouraging others to expand their artistic horizons.

'The problem with MS is that it is progressive and we have had to adapt and adapt and adapt again as my condition worsened,' Florence explains. 'People thought that changing the geography of our bathroom was some weird hobby we had because we did it so often! The disease affects the central nervous system which controls movement though it is not the nerves themselves that are affected but the sheaths covering them. No one has any idea why one is afflicted by it and as yet there is no cure.

'There is always a bit of a cloud over you that it will get worse and you wonder if you will be able to take it. I cannot deny pain exists in plenty and would like to comfort those who can't cope. Incurable progressive conditions are a burden which can crush the spirit but a wise doctor is beyond price. It is all too tempting to think that there is nothing he can do. That isn't true. Research is going on all the time but I have been guided away from fashionable "cures" and instead been given gentle sustained encouragement while the scientists get to the root of the problem.'

'I have had MS for twenty years now, but I count myself lucky that I have a supportive husband, and two caring sons, both of whom have degrees (one has a MA and the other a BA) and that they are working in their own chosen fields. And of course, there is my painting, which is deeply personal and at the same time distinctly public, for it provides me with a special viewpoint and a unique experience of life which is vital to me.

'Geoff is extremely calm – and funny. He often makes jokes about my disability. They are never in bad taste, they just make me laugh. When straightening out my cushions he will say, "One lump or two." and I remember after a particularly nice meal we had in a hotel – having to be fed in public does not deter me – I waxed philosophical and observed that life is full of peaks and troughs. Geoff, looking at my empty plate asked if this was a peak or a trough.'

'Geoff wants to keep me smiling and – Boy! – do I want to impress him!'

The Reverend Glenn Barnett

'Something more than just pictures'

'It was like being at the movies with my life story being projected on to my mind. Everything I had done wrong stood out from the rest. I remember in some sort of way calling out to God.'

Thus Glenn Barnett describes the moment when he lay drowning with a broken neck and an almost severed spinal cord. 'Those few moments were the most unusual I have ever spent. I knew I was going to drown yet I didn't panic. There was no fear, just a calmness as I inhaled the salt water.'

Glenn was born in 1947 in Port Lincoln, a typical country town in South Australia known as a major wheat port and the home of Australia's largest tuna fishing fleet. He describes himself as 'a typical country kid' of those days. He got into mischief, enjoyed roaming in the bush but best of all loved sport. At school he played football and cricket and became an athletics champion. In the 'sixties there was plenty of well paid work about and he could not wait to get out into the world and earn his own living. So at the age of fourteen he left High School to work in the spare parts department of a motor company.

The last day of November, 1962 was particularly hot and after work Glenn and a friend went to the local jetty to cool off in the sea.

After they had been swimming for an hour it was time to go for their Friday night session of table tennis.

'Like typical lazy teenagers we thought it too far to walk back along the jetty,' Glenn says. 'Instead we would take a short cut by diving in and swimming to the shore. We usually did this but tonight we were closer to the shore than usual. We climbed on to the rail and I dived after singing out our usual "Break my neck".

Those three words were a ghastly prophecy. Glenn dived twelve feet into two feet of water which being deceptively clear looked much deeper.

'I pile-dived myself into the sand at the bottom,' Glenn told the author. 'There was no pain, just a black flash. As I tried to stand up a strange tingling shot through my body and I found I could not move. I held my breath as long as I could and then began to breathe in water. Suddenly there was a lot of splashing and a boy called Graham Eastern dragged me to the shore. I thanked him but I doubt if he heard me. In fact I did not see him again for twenty-eight years when he returned to Port Lincoln on holiday with his wife. I took them out to dinner and was able to thank him properly – I have had a fantastic life and it would have been terrible to have lost it then.'

Luckily on the shore there was someone who knew what to do, packing sand round Glenn's neck to protect it until the ambulance arrived. His recollection of the events is hazy, people in a circle staring at him and then two nurses cutting away his swimming trunks in hospital and later being given liquid by means of a teapot-like object. The next day he was flown 150 miles to the Royal Adelaide Hospital where he had a tracheotomy and then an operation to graft a bone to support his broken neck.

Perhaps because he was only fifteen no one explained what had really happened to him and during the following weeks he lay in bed expecting to recover. It was only a nurse's accidental remark that broke the news to him that he would never walk again and, as he said, 'it felt as though my guts fell out'.

'There was no counselling in those days so I thought about it by myself over the weekend and I began to think that there were still things I could do in a wheelchair. Then I was transferred to the Spinal Injuries Unit at the Morris Hospital and put into a dining-room where I saw my fellow quadriplegics with their hands crippled up, and I realized I had not only lost my legs but also my arms and I felt devastated.'

At the end of a year it was decided that nothing more could be done for Glenn and he was sent home to his parents – something which filled him with dismay. In the hospital he felt secure among people disabled like himself but he was terrified of being stared at back in the world of the able-bodied.

At first he refused to go outside the house and then permitted himself to be wheeled on to the back verandah out of sight of the neighbours. It was his sister's sixteeen-year-old boy friend (now Glenn's brother-in-law) who altered all this. He invited Glenn to a friend's house and when Glenn as usual refused he grabbed the wheelchair handles and raced with it down the drive and up the road with its occupant swearing and spitting at him in frustrated fury.

As it turned out this action was one of the best experiences of Glenn's life as it broke down the barrier he was erecting against the outside world. After that he lived as normal a life as possible with friends of his own age, going out to drive-in cinemas and parties and yelling at people out of car windows – 'those stupid things that teenagers do.'

One day a little boy who was being looked after by Mrs Barnett asked Glenn to draw him a picture.

'I explained that I could not use my hands,' says Glenn. 'But next day I thought I would try with a pen in my mouth. I found it easy to draw lines fairly straight and asked mother to buy me some cheap water-colours and I began to splash around the paint. It developed slowly and I enjoyed it. In fact I felt very pleased with the results and it was only later that I realized how terrible they were. In such a situation you are encouraged with false praise when you start painting.'

In 1966 Glenn's mother had another child and because of a difficult pregnancy was unable to continue looking after him so he returned to the Morris Hospital as a long-termer.

Here he thought about life very deeply. His parents had been told that he could expect to live for about twenty-five years. How would he fill them? It seemed impossible to have a normal relationship with a member of the opposite sex, impossible to work and impossible to take part in sport which had been the most important aspect of his life.

The answer was provided by his fellow long-term patients – pleasure! This group decided that all that was left in life was pleasure which was obtained largely through alcohol.

'We got people to smuggle in booze for us,' said Glenn, 'and I often got drunk sitting in my wheelchair under the gum trees in the hospital grounds. I was taken to parties with the others and two or three times a week I would wake up with the night before a blank.'

Then, at the age of twenty, something very significant happened in his life. A new gardener came to work in the grounds. He was a Pentecostal Christian and he urged Glenn to read the New Testament. Having been taught as a boy to respect his elders Glenn complied and spent the next few months studying the Gospels.

'The result was that I felt challenged personally,' he declares. 'A radical change came over me. My whole philosophy spun round and my need for pleasure was completely altered. I saw everything in a new way from then on, even things in nature, and I became a Christian.'

At that time Glenn had begun a deep friendship with one of the nurses at the hospital, Avril Saunders, who had grown up in the Methodist faith. As their relationship deepened they discussed the question of marriage but decided that it would be out of the question, not because of Glenn's disability but because it seemed financially impossible for them to live independently as man and wife.

Ever since his mother had bought him the box of water-colours Glenn had continued to paint even through his hangover days and, having seen a television programme on a mouth-painter, he got in touch with the Association of Mouth and Foot Painting Artists. He was so encouraged at the possibility of being able to make a living out of his art that he and Avril were married in 1971 in front of a congregation made up of 175 relations and friends. He was accepted as a full member of the Association 1973 which meant that they were able to build a house in Adelaide Hills designed specially to suit a wheelchair.

Here Glenn settled down to a happy life with his wife and often painted up to eight hours a day.

'When I was at the Morris Hospital I wanted to go back to school,' he explains. 'So I was given tests to see if I had enough intelligence to study – and the result was that I was told to forget it. I was not smart enough and it would be a waste of time. But now I felt challenged by God to learn as much as I could and I began correspondence courses with Bible colleges. In 1976 I was accepted into the South Australian Bible College where alterations were actually made to the building to accommodate my wheelchair.'

After three years Glenn received his Diploma of Divinity with a distinction and was then offered a post as lecturer at the Uniting Church's Alcorn College, a lay training centre. While involved in this work he also studied to get a university degree

In studying he was given no special advantages, no extra time to sit examinations even though he had to write his papers with a pen held in his mouth. In one three-hour exam he filled eighteen foolscap pages this way.

Having gone so far in lay work Glenn now felt inspired to go further. From 1981 to 1983 he studied at Trinity College, Brisbane, and was ordained as a Minister of the Uniting Church in 1984. His first parochial work was at Bundaberg in the heart of Queensland's cane and cattle country.

In an interview on his work there, Glenn told a journalist, 'I loved parish ministry and the wheelchair presented almost no difficulties despite most Queensland houses being high-set. I could get into most of them to visit people and at those I couldn't the people were happy to come into the garden for a chat. I've been able to take weddings and funerals, even in the mud at the graveside.'

His ministry was very much a team effort with Avril acting as his chauffeur, sounding board and critic.

After Bundaberg Glenn moved to South Australia to continue his pastoral work in Port Broughton. Apart from the usual role of minister he made a point of speaking to schools and numerous community groups on disablement at which he would give demonstrations of his painting technique.

Sadly in 1989 Glenn received a severe jolt in a car in which he was travelling which affected his neck so that, despite an operation, his condition deteriorated and it became necessary for him to give up church work at the beginning of 1991. For his 'retirement' he and Avril bought a house in his home town of Port Lincoln, and here Glenn continues to paint though the amount of time he can spend on it at one time is reduced to four hours a day. This, however, has not in any way dampened his enthusiasm for art; on the contrary he is possibly more enthusiastic than ever and he gained his Master of Arts degree in 1992.

'I find painting totally fulfilling,' he declares. 'And I see it as something more than just pictures because I believe art stimulates peoples' thoughts about reality. I am often told that I must be at peace with myself because my work demonstrates peace, and I think that's true.

'I paint mainly landscapes, travelling all over Australia with Avril to get subjects and camping out in the heart of the bush. My greatest love is the Flinders Ranges – they are magnificent with very splendid colours and I keep going back to them.'

In talking to Glenn one finds that while the conversation may be serious it never strays far from humour. A discussion on philosophy might suddenly turn into an anecdote on how at his sister's wedding something went wrong with the portable plumbing required through his disability with the result that as his wheelchair progressed down the church it left a trickle the length of the aisle – or how on his first day at a parish in Queensland the lifting device to help him out of the car broke and sent him sprawling full length at the feet of the minister he was going to work with.

Back on the philosophical side he says, 'I am one of those strange people who can never accept my disability. To me it is silly to say I accept it – of course I would rather be able to walk! You adjust to rather than accept disability, and I have managed to do this through my art work and as a Christian. Avril and I have had a happy and amazing life together and we could not have done this without me being able to earn my living as an artist.'

JOHN BUNCE *Floral Abundance* Watercolour 35 x 25 cm

JOHN BUNCE
Little Dog
Tempera 42 x 40 cm

JOHN BUNCE *Cold Winter* Watercolour 38 x 48 cm

FLORENCE BUNN *Little Town* Ceramic 15 x 20 cm

JOHN BUNCE
Mother & Child
Oil 55 x 45 cm

FLORENCE BUNN
Winter Landscape
Watercolour   20 x 14 cm

FLORENCE BUNN
Suburban Garden
Watercolour   23 x 18 cm

44

GLENN BARNETT
Roosting for the Evening
Oil   30 x 20 cm

Overleaf: GLENN BARNETT
Coming from Bullyache
Oil   30 x 41 cm

GLENN BARNETT
Landscape
Acrylic   25 x 36 cm

45

WENDY BARBER   *Children's Alphabet*

WENDY BARBER
The Kiss
Watercolour   34 x 25 cm

48

RUTH CHRISTENSEN   *Trees in Autumn*   Oil   18 x 27 cm

RUTH CHRISTENSEN   *Summer Idyll*   Oil   40 x 50 cm

RUTH CHRISTENSEN   *Flower Market*   Watercolour   34 x 24 cm

RUTH CHRISTENSEN   *At the Sea*   Watercolour 36 x 24 cm

RUTH CHRISTENSEN *Roses* Oil 41 x 33 cm

STEVEN CHAMBERS
Walk on the Beach
Watercolour   40 x 35 cm

STEVEN CHAMBERS
Snowbound
Watercolour   40 x 50 cm

JOY CLARKE
Companions
Watercolour   25 x 18 cm

JOY CLARKE
Spring Visitor
Watercolour

JOY CLARKE *On the Toadstool* Watercolour

PAUL DRIVER
Schooner
Oil   51 x 61 cm

PAUL DRIVER   *American Frigate*   Oil

55

PAUL DRIVER
Winter Sun
Oil   51 x 61 cm

PAUL DRIVER   *Walking*   Oil   41 x 51 cm

Wendy Barber

'I needed to survive.'

In the window of Wendy Barber's home is a sign announcing 'Honey for sale' – a sign which is puzzling to anyone who arrives at the house in search of a disabled artist. Yet the keeping of bees is just one of the many facets of Wendy's extraordinary life, reflecting her love of nature which in turn is reflected in her paintings produced by a brush held painfully in her mouth.

Wendy's interest in art was fostered early by her father, a Fleet Street printer and later in life a television engineer whose hobby was pencil drawing, and this was furthered when she attended art school. At the age of nineteen she married and two years later gave birth to her son Matthew. Shortly afterwards it was found that she was suffering from cancer of the throat and neck.

Wendy's mother looked after the baby while she spent the first of many long periods in hospital.

'The specialist told me that I was more likely to die than live,' Wendy recalls, 'but after three months in hospital receiving intensive treatment and major surgery I was allowed home two days before Matthew's first birthday. At that time my greatest anxiety was fearing that my husband would not be able to cope with the cancer. In fact he left me when Matthew was two years old.

'The way I survived was not to think of negative things, and I needed to survive for Matthew's sake. If you have a child there's a bond there, and in between my times in hospital I tried to stay as well as I could so I could carry on looking after him. Then three years after I had been told I had cancer, Matthew contracted meningitis. I did not have time to think about my illness, all I could think was, "I have to cope. There is no choice." and it was at times like that when you find you have strengths that you didn't know you had.'

The illness left the little boy brain-damaged with severe deafness and epilepsy, yet thanks to Wendy's devotion he has grown up to be a fine young man who is able to lead an independent life and gives much of his free time to voluntary work with the Scout Association.

After seven years of treatment which included three major operations Wendy was declared clear of cancer. It had been an almost miraculous recovery and yet she did not feel as well as she ought. Before long she began losing her balance and falling over, and soon she could only move about like a young child sliding on its bottom. Then it was discovered that she was a victim of multiple sclerosis, the diagnosis of which had been delayed because all her symptoms had been put down to cancer.

Today Wendy is paralysed from the shoulders down and suffers a great deal of pain caused by inflammation of the spinal cord compounded by arthritis in the head, jaw, neck and spine, and by trigeminal neuralgia which causes pain in her mouth and face. Yet her will to fight back has increased in ratio to her illness.

Before she was confined to a wheelchair in 1978 Wendy enrolled with the Open University to become an educational psychologist. It took seven years of study to qualify for her degree – often she got up at four in the morning to keep up with her schedule – but the result was that today she has children referred to her for remedial work.

'This work began some years ago, when the child of one of my helpers was in trouble and needed help, and since then many disadvantaged and handicapped children have been sent for sessions with me,' she says. 'The fact that I conduct them from a wheelchair does not seem to matter and now I have extended my studies and am reading for my Master's degree in child and eductional psychology.

'One thing that made me happy about getting my degree was that my father knew about it just before he died. There was a write-up in a newspaper about me with a photograph which I took to show him in hospital and he was absolutely thrilled. Sadly, my mother had died eleven months earlier but she knew I would do it.

'Nobody could have been more supportive than my parents and when Mummy died there was so much grief and emotion I had to get out of me – you can only cry so much and I had a child of fourteen to think of – that I decided I had to do something positive. I had to make use of the intense feelings within me, and so I began writing – it had to be about something beautiful, peaceful and about the good that is around us in the world.'

Wendy commenced a book on natural history and gardening, using a computer to get down the words and at that early stage illustrating by hand. Half-way through she lost the use of her fingers and arms and had to change to painting with a brush held in her mouth just as she used a mouthstick to operate the computer keyboard.

'The book was my phoenix, something good and positive that came out of my grief,' she says. 'I had to try and be happy. It was a responsibility to my parents after all they had done for me.'

Wendy's gardening book is now complete after five years' work. She says that it does have a slant towards those with problems, the first chapter is about being handicapped but not necessarily physically, mentally or emotionally.

'You can be handicapped if you live in a bedsit and haven't got a garden and you want to grow an apple tree,' she declares. 'I have described things to make and do, adventurous things if you are hale and hearty and with money in the bank to buy materials, and – based on my own experience – there are things to do that don't need money and which are possible even if you are not well.

'When I was a child I used to write stories – imaginative rubbish! Dad would say something suitable and fatherly and then add, "Wendy, if you want to write anything that anyone will read you must write something about what you know." And that's what I have tried to do. I like writing. If you don't have anyone to tell things to you can tell them to your computer – and it doesn't interrupt you.'

At first Wendy found the technique of mouth-painting very difficult but she was so desperate to illustrate her book that forced herself to carry on. One of her problems was that the mouthstick was too heavy and exhausting because of the arthritis in her jaw, and when she saw a painting by the well-known mouth-painter Charles Fowler she wrote to him for advice.

Apart from practical help, Charles told her about the Association of Mouth and Foot Painting Artists and suggested that when she had done six paintings she thought were reasonable she should submit them to the organisation. This she did at the beginning of 1989 and in June 1989 she was accepted as a student, the stipend she receives helping her to maintain her hard won independence.

This independence is symbolized by Wendy's house – The Beehive – in Kent. Here she lives alone, with much of her equipment operated by mouth, though she might not look at it that way as she has the company of a high-spirited young labrador bitch named Merryweather. Because she is so disabled she requires the services of helpers, and has a rota of thirteen regulars and six who are standbys in case of emergency, such as when a regular might ring up and say 'I've got flu so I dare not come near you.'

Wendy admits that it has been a fight to retain her right to lead a life of her own.

'I had to come off the Social Services because I am what they call too "cost dependent", she says. 'It meant that by staying at home I needed more help than average and this was not fair to the others so I was told that I must go into residential care. I fought a great battle to remain in my own home, and from the Social Services' point of view I lost it because they were able to withdraw their assistance and continue saying that I should be in residential care. On the other hand I won in that I am still in my house and coping by employing my own carers.

'I receive no care help from the Social Services now and I pay my helpers myself – much easier since I joined the Mouth and Foot Painting Artists – and I shall stay in my own home as long as I possibly can.

'When I moved to this house, which is specially adapted for my electric wheelchair, I called it The Beehive because my parents had always called the homes we lived in by that name – from the B in Barber, my maiden name – and I carried on the tradition. Then people asked me, "Do you keep bees?" and I began to think "Why not?" I had always enjoyed bees and one day four years ago I said to Matthew, "I'm going to keep bees." And I waited. "Good!" he said and, unlike everyone else, he did not ask me how was I going to manage.'

Wendy managed by employing a boy, a tyro beekeeper, to follow her instructions and now has a double hive which she designed herself housing 50,000 bees at the bottom of her patio garden. Despite the 'Honey for sale' notice most of the honey produced is given away.

One of the problems of the paralysed is that they cannot brush away insects that land upon them, yet this does not trouble Wendy when she visits the hive.

'The bees know me,' she explains. 'They recognise the wheelchair and when they see it they say, "Here comes Wendy", and they sit on it which I find very pleasant. They never harm me though I do keep my mouth closed.'

Wendy's constant companion is Merryweather the Labrador who is utterly devoted to her mistress with whom she has lived since she was a six-week old puppy. Most of all she provides that rich bond of companionship between animal and human enjoyed by several other artists mentioned in this book.

Looking out on to the patio garden, with its flowers and bees, is Wendy's studio. Here everything is designed for an artist confined to a wheelchair, and here she spends her happiest hours with the devoted Merryweather beside her. She paints mostly in water-colour, though she does sometimes use oils and coloured pencils.

'I paint in my head first,' she explains. 'I spend a long time building up the picture stroke by stroke in my mind. I need to know exactly where I am going with a picture because of the proximity of the paper to my nose when I actually paint. I need to hold a picture in my memory because executing it can be difficult – it takes me between two and three hundred hours to paint one.

'I sometimes have to cope with two opposing wishes,' she adds. 'My body wants me to stop painting and my brain wants me to keep on.'

Apart from pain-killing drugs, Wendy uses an electronic device based on acupuncture which sends an alternative current down the spine to alleviate the pain enough for her to be able to continue painting. Yet there is no hint of her difficulties in her clear bright paintings which usually depict animals and birds, the natural history subjects that she has always loved, as well as traditional subjects for greeting cards.

'I am now determined to become a full member of the Association,' Wendy says, 'and I'm so busy with my work that I don't have time to think about me – you survive that way. And I very much believe you should put more back into life than you take out, not for any commendable reason but self-preservation – you cannot be happy if you take out more than you are prepared to give.'

Ruth Christensen

'Strength from the struggle'

In 1992 the Council of Europe announced that its official Christmas card for that year would be designed by a mouth or foot painter. In response twenty-one members of the Association of Mouth and Foot Painting Artists submitted a total of sixty-two designs and the work of three was short-listed: Ruth Christensen of Denmark, Wendy Barber of England and Klaus Spahni of Switzerland.

When the final painting was chosen it was Ruth Christensen's 'Christmas in Europe', a snow scene in which merry tots in Santa Claus costumes pull a sledge loaded with lettered building blocks that spell out 'Europa-Europe.'

As a result hundreds of thousands of people world-wide became aware that 'art without hands' is not only possible but can be highly professional.

This aspect of the competition pleased Ruth Christensen most as she is an enthusiastic worker on behalf of her fellow disabled painters, especially those in Scandinavia whom she represents after being elected an AMFPA Board member in 1993. Not only does she travel to the Association's headquarters in Vaduz twice a year to confer with the other Board members in the Association's 'Parliament' but, in company with her sister Lis, she tours the Nordic countries visiting artists to discuss their ideas and well-being.

When Ruth was eleven years old she was enjoying a cycle ride with a friend one day when she approached a level crossing notorious for its poor visibility. She pedalled on to it, had a fleeting impression of a locomotive looming above her... then nothing.

Ruth has no memory of the actual accident which she still finds difficult to discuss – only coming round in a hospital bed to discover that both her arms had been severed above the elbow. It was the beginning of a long fight to regain the normal expectations of life that seemed to have ended at the level crossing.

'It was a hard struggle but one gains strength from having to struggle like I did,' she says today.

Ruth was born in 1929 at Lynge in Nordsjälland.

'I had a wonderful country childhood,' she told the author when he met her at an AMFPA conference in Vaduz. 'There were five of us children and we were a very happy family – indeed we are still very close and meet often, and that has been a great strength to me. Lis, who accompanies me on my travels, is my older sister, there is a younger brother and then a set of twins.

'You can imagine how my accident cast a shadow over our lives that up until then had been so carefree. That was one of the reasons why, when I came out of hospital, I was determined to get back to as normal a life as possible. I really struggled to manage with everyday things, and gradually I began to succeed.

'I used my mouth to put on my doll's clothes, turn the pages of my book and I tried to write holding a pen in my teeth which was far from easy. The good thing was that I was able to keep going to my usual school. My father made an appliance which, attached to what remained of my upper arms, enabled me to use a fork so that I was no longer dependant on someone feeding me.

'My father was a very inventive man. In Nordsjälland he had a small repair garage but when the war began cars were hardly used so the business naturally declined and he had to look for some other means of livelihood. The result was that he turned to invention and began to design various machines which he then manufactured. And so he coped.'

And in her own life Ruth coped by trying to fulfil her childhood ambition to become an artist. After she had completed her school course she applied to be enrolled in an art school in Copenhagen but was bitterly disappointed by the response she received.

'When it was discovered that I had no hands I was told that it would be impossible for me to take the course – it would be far too difficult for someone without hands.'

In reply Ruth demonstrated her ability to draw with mouth-held pens and pencils – and was accepted. She commuted by train to Copenhagen for her lessons until the family moved to the capital, buying a house in the Vanlîse suburb where Ruth lives today.

After art college Ruth's standard of drawing was good enough for her to get work in various advertising agencies.

'I did all sorts of work – brochures, catalogues and advertisements and I created fabric designs for a linen manufacturer,' she says. 'It seemed that I had got over my handicap in that I was living a more active life than most. In 1960 I went to Canada to work in an advertising agency in Montreal.'

Looking back on her life Ruth recalls this period as one of the most exciting. She learned a lot, was surrounded by friends with whom she travelled in the USA and fell in love with the man she hoped to marry. The wedding took place in Copenhagen in 1964.

Ruth and her husband bought a house in Nordsjälland where to Ruth's huge delight her son Thomas was born.

Meanwhile she continued to freelance as an advertising artist which was to be of benefit when the marriage ended after nine years. Ruth returned to Copenhagen with Thomas and moved into the upper storey of her parents' house.

'During the years while my son was still small it was a struggle to get by financially,' she says. 'In my parents' home I had a built-on studio for my freelance work.'

The break-through in Ruth's career came when the MFK – the Danish branch of the mouth and foot painting artists' association – heard about her work and offered her a scholarship. In 1982 she became a full member of the MFK and three years later, following the death of the founder Erich Stegmann, she attended the Association's congress in Vaduz where Marlyse Tovae was elected as the new president. There Ruth met the Swedish artists Sune Fick and Elof Lundberg whose cheerful enthusiasm she found greatly encouraging.

'To become a member of such a partnership and receive a regular income was a marvellous lifting of my problems,' says Ruth. 'It has made it possible for me to develop my own painting as it was always my ambition to do. Working in my own way gives me freedom.

'In the beginning when it came to painting I wanted to do everything correctly – to paint everything exactly the way it looked but as I learned more I dared to go my own way. That is what I mean by freedom.

'Of course I get ideas from actual things. I like to go about Copenhagen with my sketch pad and into the park to see the trees, and into exhibitions of course. Then when I get back to my studio I look at my sketches and let my imagination have full rein. When I decide what to do I make a drawing on the canvas, begin to apply the colour and then the painting goes its own way. Although I have a feeling as to how the picture will be when I start, it never seems to come out that way. It is as though something takes over.'

It seems to Ruth that her work develops a life of its own in the way that some writers believe their characters form their own independent personalities.

'Although I like to work with water colours best I find that by switching to different mediums and trying new techniques I do not get stale,' Ruth explains. 'For this reason I try to use oil paints sometimes but I find the pigment heavy. When I do use oils I do so as if they are water colours, applying them in thin transparent layers which are easy to work over. Usually I have several paintings in progress at any one time and I work on them until something tells me they are complete, if not I give up at a certain stage and begin on something fresh.'

One motif that has long fascinated Ruth is that of a glass flower vase with light streaming through and a view of a room behind distorted by light refraction. It is one of the hardest subjects for an artist to tackle but she has returned to it many times.

The many greetings cards that Ruth has painted are not only known in Scandinavia but are published internationally and she believes that a key to her success is the fact that she has worked as an advertising artist – the message of her cards is direct and people respond to it immediately.

In Denmark each year a competition is held for artists to submit ideas for Christmas postage stamps. In 1982 Ruth was chosen as the winner and again in 1988 when her picture of a little angel appeared on a stamp.

Looking back on her life Ruth is adamant that she has 'had it good'.

'Life is certainly easier for me than most of the other members of the Association in that I can walk freely,' she admits. 'I am able to use a car with the help of special steering equipment and in the summer I spend time in a house on the coast which charges my creative batteries. I am also very lucky in that I am on close terms with my family, with my son Thomas and my little grandson Marcus who is a joy to have as a model. Best of all is the fact that I have the opportunity to paint without economic pressure. It is painting that I want to continue with for as long as I am capable of working.

'Although I have a belief I am not one that goes to church but I think I have to thank someone for all that I have got.'

Steven Chambers

'Willpower and my Mum!'

Arthrogypoesis is the name of the rare and mysterious condition which afflicted Steven Chambers. He believes that there are only twenty others who share his ailment in Great Britain. The cause of arthrogypoesis is not known but its effect upon Steven was that he was born with his arms complete in every way except one – they were without muscles. The condition was further complicated by the painful stiffening of the leg joints. At the Great Ormond Hospital for Sick Children his mother and father were told that it was most unlikely that he would ever walk.

It was a pronouncement that Steven's mother refused to accept. During the periods he was out of hospital she continuously massaged his legs and made him do exercises to strengthen his lower limbs though nothing could be done for his arms which hung uselessly at his sides. It was then that she showed the determination which has been a key factor in her son's life.

'She used to take me into the garden and prop me up on my feet against a wall,' says Steven as though explaining a humorous episode. 'Then she would leave me so that I was stranded there. This used to happen every day until I got so fed up with it that I began to take steps and from then on I actually started walking. The fact that I can walk about today is due to willpower and my Mum!'

For a while the child had to wear callipers and later Steven underwent an operation to have a weak knee joint 'fused' into a permanent position in order to bear his weight and there is the possibility that he might require a similar operation on his other knee later on.

Until he was sixteen Steven was in and out of hospital but this did not hamper his education.

'I went to an ordinary school,' he explains, 'and there I was accepted as an ordinary person. I was never treated as though I was disabled. I think that this was due to the attitude my mother and father instilled in me – to always carry on as though I was not handicapped. Of course there were a lot of things I could not do and I had to accept that and make the best of what I could do.'

When Steven was unable to attend school his teachers took it in turns to visit him in hospital with his lessons so he would not be behind when he returned to class. They also went to his home when he had exams coming after he broke his leg. This came about when his friends announced they were going into the woods near his home in Denham, Middlesex. His father warned him not to go with them, saying it would be dangerous because the ground was full of holes covered by long grass. But Steven loved the outdoors and the thought of his friends having fun among the trees was too much for the boy. As soon as he could get out of sight of his family he joined them in the woods and proved the truth of his father's words by tripping over and breaking his leg.

From the beginning Steven used his mouth to hold a pencil – 'Not difficult because I had never known anything different.' What did frustrate him was that often he could not get the effects with it that he wanted.

'I had a very short temper as a child,' he admits. 'Sometimes I would throw down the pen in a rage, and my mother would make me carry on until I could do what I set out to. Once I wanted to cut some paper with a pair of scissors but it seemed an impossible task. "You just sit until you work out a way to do it," my mother said and she left me alone in the room. Somehow or other I finally managed to hold one of the scissors' handles in my mouth and work the blades along the paper which lay flat on the table. Since then I have always managed to cut my own paper.'

Perhaps because his grandfather was an artist Steven enjoyed art classes while at school though at the time he had no ambition to become a professional painter. When he left school at the age of eighteen he hoped to get employment on computers in the Martin Baker Ejection Seat Company where his father was a designer but to his intense disappointment this did not materialize.

'So I went to art college for something to do,' he says 'There was a nurse who took an interest in me and my work, and in 1980 she suggested that I got in touch with the Association of Mouth and Foot Painting Artists. I sent in some of my work and two weeks later I was offered a studentship.'

Since then he has continued to live with his family and develop his art work. So far the two things of which he is most proud is that his work was shown in a Canadian exhibition and a rabbit character which he painted for children was well received in Japan.

To begin with Steven painted in oils but like some other mouth painters he found these too difficult and now he uses water-colours.

'It is so much easier to clean a brush by rinsing it in a jar of water than having to clean oil from the bristles with turps,' he says. What frustrates him with art work sometimes is not the technique of painting but the question of inspiration. On some occasions he will get his art materials out only to find that after an hour he puts them away without a line being drawn. At other times the reverse is true. When the creative urge is upon him he paints right through the night and is surprised when day breaks. He particularly likes drawing animals and apart from his straightforward work he loves to let his imagination run wild.

Steven's penchant for fantasy finds reign as a make-up artist. For many years his brother has been an addict of the game 'Dungeons and Dragons' in which each player takes on the role of a character in an amazingly complicated fantasy world such as one might find in the works of J.R.R. Tolkien. Since boyhood he played this game with a group of friends and now that they have grown up they have taken the game further and actually act it out. Each member of the group takes it in turn to be 'dungeon master' and map out the nature of the forthcoming game and then the players, fully costumed and equipped as the character they portray, take to the woods. The rules are very strict; for example they cannot take modern food with them but must survive on fruit and home-baked bread. A flask of water is the only drink allowed.

Not only do they dress like characters in these role plays but they make-up like them – no doubt to the surprise of unsuspecting visitors to the woodland! Here Steven's skill comes into use making up the players as elves, halflings, dwarves and so on. He also designs their costumes.

On top of this Steven works on the most unusual 'canvas' of any mouth painter – the bodies of cars. Fascinated by cars himself, he is in great demand by enthusiasts whose hobby is the customizing of VW Beetles to decorate them with his designs. Although he cannot drive, his interest in cars extends to making the most exquisite and detailed models which are then lovingly painted. At first thought it seems impossible that such miniatures could be the work of a man who has no other means of assembling them than with his mouth yet Steven uses his lips to hold the tiny pieces and to use the special glue to bond them together. He remarks cheerfully that the only thing he has to watch is that 'I don't swallow the bits.'

For someone who has no use in his arms and who was once thought to be incapable of walking, Steven has a wide range of interests which includes his unusual pets such as the

Australian lizards who grew so big they had to be finally domiciled in the conservatory. These days his animal friends consist of a parrot, two gerbils, a dog which is a cross between a Labrador and an Alsation, and a delightful chinchilla who loves to perch on his shoulder. When one touches her it becomes obvious why the beautifully soft grey chinchilla fur was so prized by furriers.

Next to painting Steven's favourite occupation is night fishing.

'I fish with my brother in a local lake,' he says. 'it is surrounded by woodland and the wildlife is marvellous. We go there in the evening and walk about the shore and then settle down for fishing at about 9 o'clock. What I love about it is the peace. And as far as the actual fishing is concerned I can do everything except take the fish off the hook. I use a very light rod which is well balanced and my father made a nylon mouthpiece which enables me to hold it.'

When the author first visited Steven it was just three weeks after his marriage. His wife Jo, who enthusiastically shares his many interests, was a children's nanny and had only known Steven six weeks when they began discussing the question of marriage.

'We talked it over one weekend and decided that this was what we both wanted,' Steven recalls. 'I went home and announced that I was going to be married and my family said "Fine!" and by Tuesday night I had made arrangements with the church, booked a hall for the reception, bought the rings and got myself a new suit. And the wedding was a fantastic family affair.' Now the couple are the proud parents of two children.

Despite arthrogypoesis Steven Chambers has built up a full life for himself and now there remains only one goal. 'My ambition,' he says, 'is to become a full member of the Association.'

Joy Clarke

'I set to work as best I could ...'

Disabled artists often gain inspiration for their work from things they loved in the days when they were fit and mobile – Paul Driver with marine scenes, Bruce Peardon with the Australian bush – and Joy Clarke with flowers. Her studies of delicate and detailed flower arrangements are painted with a love for growing things that goes back to the days when young Joy worked in a garden nursery.

It was not an occupation that she had planned; indeed she had started an A-Level course at school when circumstances forced her to give up her studies and take a job – she chose horticulture because of her interest in plants – in order to keep her mother's home going.

During Joy's childhood in Parkestone, Dorset, her mother suffered from a very rare neurological disease known as Charcot-Marie Tooth Syndrome. Despite the effect of her mother's illness on Joy and her brother, she says that she loved living in Dorset and had a good childhood.

'Then, when I was sixteen, I realized that there was something not quite right with me,' she says. 'I was still at school and I found that I could not do things in the gym that once came easily. After a school medical I was sent to an orthopaedic surgeon because my feet were painful and had become an awful shape.'

Although her mother's illness had begun with her feet, it did not occur to Joy that the Charcot-Marie Tooth Syndrome could be hereditary. Nor did her mother want to believe that she had passed on such a serious complaint to her daughter.

'Having suffered so much herself, she could not accept the fact that there was anything really wrong with me,' Joy explains. 'She wanted to ignore it, and I think she was quite firm if not rude to the surgeon who wanted to do something about my feet and the matter was dropped.'

Soon after this Joy had to get to work because her mother's condition worsened and she was without the support of a husband. For a year the girl worked in a nursery by day and spent the rest of her time looking after her mother who, as her illness progressed, became increasingly difficult.

'A time came when I could no longer cope with earning enough to keep the home going and looking after her, especially as her illness had affected her mentally,' Joy says. The problem was solved when Joy's mother was able to go and live in a Cheshire Home in Hampshire while Joy and her brother went to stay with relatives in Rugby where Joy found more horticultural work which she loved. During the day she wore Wellingtons which she changed for slippers when she got home, the sad fact being that she could no longer wear shoes.

Before long she had to go into hospital for an operation which seemed successful and, confident of her future, she got married at the age of twenty-one. Then the benefit of the operation wore off and after more tests it was found that she was suffering from the same neurological condition as her mother, with the added complication of a circulatory complaint.

The progress of the illness was almost imperceptible over the following years and Joy did manage to lead a reasonably normal life, giving birth to her daughter when she was twenty-seven and to her son a year later. Marital problems began to throw a shadow over her family life, and when she was thirty Joy was forced to seek a divorce. For the next three years she looked after the two children alone which became more and more difficult as the disease advanced and forced her to use crutches.

Looking back on that difficult time, Joy says, 'It was terrible when the children were little and I had to send them up to bed alone. I just could not get upstairs to tuck them in and kiss them goodnight.'

Joy's condition worsened dramatically in 1977 and, after being admitted to hospital, she realized she would not be able to look after her children in the future and steeled herself to make arrangements for having them fostered. It was the same heartbreaking decision that Heather Strudwick had faced twenty years earlier. And Joy's spirits were further lowered in the September of the following year when it was found necessary to amputate her leg. In 1980 her other leg had to be removed and, to make matters even worse, her ability to use her arms and hands was failing.

When the doctors decided there was nothing more they could do for her, the problem was what to be done with someone in her condition. It seemed that because of the nature of her illness she did not fit neatly into any particular category and as a result found herself being moved from pillar to post. Despite the fact that she was still a young woman she spent two years in a geriatric hospital and, although her complaint was neurological in nature and she was now paralysed, she ended up in the corner of a ward devoted to cardiac cases.

She remembers that she was miserable for weeks. In looking after the cardiac cases the staff were far too busy to attend to her, and sometimes she would lie for half a day waiting for a drink. Having reached a stage where she could no longer turn the page of a book, she found it impossible to escape her surroundings by reading as she had in the past.

Hope was renewed when she managed to get herself sent to the Mary Marlborough Lodge, a residential unit attached to the Nuffield Orthopaedic Hospital just outside Oxford, and here she was provided with an electric wheelchair which she could control with the small amount of movement in her left hand. Three months later this movement was lost, and once more Joy was confined to bed. She finally found herself in the Hospital of St. Cross in Rugby. Here, in 1982, the registrar who was anxious about Joy and the seemingly aimless life she was forced to lead, suggested to her that she should do something with her time – such as writing or drawing.

Although she now had no use in her arms, the idea seized Joy's imagination and with the aid of the occupational therapist she was strapped into a wheelchair for hour-long periods while she endeavoured to come to terms with a piece of paper pinned to hardboard, a box of children's water-colours and a brush that was placed in her mouth.

'I set to work as best I could and the first thing that I did was a Christmas card with a candle and a piece of holly round the bottom,' she recalls. 'Although I say it myself it was good – had it been awful I would never have tried again.'

Christmas was seven weeks away and Joy decided that this year she would paint her own cards. In order to do this she forced herself to spend longer and longer strapped painfully in her wheelchair but she achieved her aim and by the middle of December she had produced twenty-six cards, a few that she particularly liked she decided to keep for herself.

As it turned out this was a fortunate decision. Joy's therapist told her that she ought to contact the Association of Mouth and Foot Painting Artists. Joy only knew of them because her mother used to buy their cards and the thought that they might be interested in her seemed ludicrous.

'I had only been painting for three months,' she explains, 'and I could not do anything large because I was unable to control long-handled brushes, and because of the nature of my disability I do not have the reach for wide pictures.'

Nevertheless the therapist had her way and a reply came from the Association asking for some samples of Joy's work. How thankful she was that she had kept some of her cards which impressed the Association's panel of judges so much that despite the short time she had been painting she was invited to become a student. Two years later she was made a full member.

'Joining the Association was a turning point for me,' Joy says. 'Apart from anything else it meant I could save up to buy my present electric wheelchair, the seat of which was made for me at the Mary Marlborough Lodge in Oxford. It enabled me to sit up for long periods – which gradually became all day – in relative comfort and in an orthopaedically correct position.'

And after being adrift for so long in different hospitals Joy realized her dream of independence by moving into her own home in Rugby where Social Services found her a disused bungalow which stood in the grounds of what had once been a home for the elderly. Despite its neglected appearance she fell in love with it at first sight, no doubt because its weed-filled garden awakened her horticultural instincts.

Today the bungalow has been transformed into a delightful home which Joy shares with a large number of house plants. When she first moved in there was no furniture or carpet but a grant from the Association helped her to furnish it. In her special electric chair – controlled by a mechanism activated by pressure from her chin – Joy is able to travel from room to room and position herself in front of her easel for work sessions in the spare room which is now a studio.

Joy happily lives on her own with nurses coming in the morning to get her up and in the evening to put her to bed, and three mornings a week a helper comes in from the Crossroads scheme to do the housework. Her great delight is the garden she has created from a wilderness. Obviously it is impossible for her to do the physical work herself and she has to employ someone to do it for her, but she has the fun of planning it and going out to buy the plants in her electric wheelchair.

One of the pleasures of having her own home again is that she can entertain her children who visit her regularly and do their bit in the garden when there is weeding or planting to be done. The flowers grown there are often the inspiration for her paintings and she says, 'You have to love the things you paint.'

Since she moved into the bungalow and proved that she is capable of an independent life Joy still has had problems to face. She has to take drugs each day to keep pain at bay, and she has been to hospital for more operations, yet she somehow retains an enthusiasm for life that shines through in her delicate paintings.

Paul Driver

Under full sail

Paul Driver is an artist who draws his inspiration from the things he loved before he became disabled – the sea and the vessels that sail upon it. Speaking of his life as a young man he says, 'I learned to sail a dinghy on the River Blackwater and spent many holidays on the Norfolk Broads. Sailing was to me the purest pleasure I knew, whether I was trying in a dinghy to coax steerage way from an almost non-existent breeze or hanging on the shuddering tiller of a thirty-footer with the sails full and the wash rushing past the hull. I often thought of my boyhood when, passionately fond of the sea even then, I longed to sail in a windjammer.'

In 1944, at the age of eighteen, Paul had volunteered to join the navy, but to his horror he found that instead of becoming a sailor the authorities, in the form of the Ministry of Labour, decided that he must become a Bevin Boy.

Bevin Boys – they got their nickname from the then Minister of Labour Ernest Bevin – were conscripted to work in mines to maintain Britain's coal production. Originally men were given the choice of going into the services or the coalfields but as most men preferred the idea of a rifle to a pick, a ballot system was introduced so that a fifth of recruits were drafted to the coalfields.

A disappointed Paul was given a month's training at Creswell Colliery and then sent to the mining village of Eastwood on the Derbyshire border where he worked underground driving pit ponies.

He remained a Bevin Boy for three years during which he used his free time to explore by bicycle the countryside around Nottingham and the Peak District. And after his term as a miner ended the love of the countryside persisted.

Looking back on his twenties as the good years, Paul says, 'At the beginning I had little money but the things I liked doing – cycling, walking, staying at youth hostels – were not expensive. Alone, or with my younger brother, I covered a large part of England on my bicycle. With friends from my mining days – and some of the friendships I formed then have lasted until today – I visited France and Scotland, and there were long walking tours in Wales, Cornwall and the Lake District.'

And, of course, sailing.

After leaving the pits Paul worked as a clerk in a City office – a job 'boring beyond belief' – and then, having started training as a quantity surveyor before he became a Bevin Boy, he returned to that profession with the London County Council Housing Department. Later he moved to a private firm that had just opened up a new office in Leeds which gave him access to the Yorkshire Moors and the Pennines.

In 1955 a Poliomyelitis epidemic spread through Britain. When Paul first felt 'under the weather' he dismissed the symptoms as being those of 'flu, but when he collapsed his landlady called a doctor and within an hour the young man was in the Seacroft Hospital. By now he had to fight for breath and he guessed that the had contracted polio when he was told that he would have to be put in an iron lung. For the next year he remained a prisoner of the machine which kept him alive through its constantly changing air pressure inflating and deflating his lungs.

To pass the time he read a great deal. His head protruded from an airtight collar and books were placed open on a glass shelf fitted above his face. But what absorbed him more than books was having an Ordnance Survey map on the shelf so that he followed the lines of well remembered paths and in imagination once more saw the landscapes he loved.

Paul's progress was better than expected and he worked at using his throat muscles to breathe until it was possible for him to be independent of the lung for periods of eight hours.

He explains, 'I normally breathe with the remaining muscles in the front and side of my neck – the muscles you would use if you were taking extra deep breath. Glossopharengeal breathing ("frog breathing" which is used by Heather Strudwick) is a separate process. It consists of trapping small amounts of air with the soft palate, forcing it down into the lungs and holding it there by closing the larynx then repeating the process several times so that the chest is pumped up rather like a bicycle tyre. I do not depend on frog breathing but use it when I need a bit more breath or when I need an extra deep breath such as when I cough.'

Next Paul was transferred to Pinderfields Orthopaedic Hospital where he was given special exercises and began to use a rubber-tipped rod attached to a head harness to turn the pages of his books. Eighteen months after he was taken ill he was able to return to sleeping in an ordinary bed in which he wore a portable respirator while during the day he was able to sit up in a wheelchair. He was moved to the Western Hospital in Fulham, London, so that he could be near his parents, and when his brother got married in the summer of 1957 he was able to attend the wedding.

Although almost completely paralysed at first, the remaining movement in his legs and feet was improved by physiotherapy. Earlier on Paul had cherished an ambition to be an author, and now this was revived when he began to write with a ballpoint pen which, fixed in a bobbin, he was able to hold between his first and second toe. However this method was slow and he changed to using a typewriter the keys of which he pressed with a piece of dowelling taped to his big toe.

The next breakthrough was an apparatus which enabled him to feed himself.

'By a strange coincidence it was invented in New Zealand for a man who not only had the same problem as me but the same surname – Driver,' Paul says. 'Jim Driver, whom I later learned was a member of the Association of Mouth and Foot Painting Artists, had a "Distaff". It consisted of a thin metal arm mounted on a metal tube which the user could operate by means of a foot pedal. I cannot tell you what a great delight it was to be able to sit at a dining table and eat under my own steam after having been fed by nurses for so long.'

Although Paul had found it difficult to write with a ballpoint between his toes, he discovered he could use a brush effectively which enabled him to take up painting as a hobby. His early efforts were understandably crude but he was eager to improve and progressed so well that a hospital chaplain took several of his pictures along to an exhibition at the local library. On hearing of the way that these paintings had been produced, a reporter wrote an article on them for his newspaper. This item finally reached the Association of Mouth and Foot Painting Artists and Paul was asked to submit specimens of his artwork.

Because he felt his painting was too amateurish Paul declined the invitation.

In 1960 he went for a year to the Mary Marlborough Lodge, the new Nuffield Orthopaedic Centre in Oxford, which had been established to assist the disabled to make the most of whatever movement they retained. Here, together with another "upside down" polio (a name given to polio victims who have lost the use of their arms but retained some use in their legs), he devised a sucessful conversion to enable them to operate a hand controlled electric wheelchair – a piece of string. When this period was over he went to live at the Athol House Cheshire Home in Upper Norwood which was close to his parents' despite having worked so hard at it but, as though to compensate for this, he found that his painting had progressed until it was something more serious than a hobby. He remembered the interest the Association of Mouth and Foot Painting Artists had shown in him some years earlier and now he had confidence enough to send in some samples of his work for evaluation by the Association's artistic panel.

In 1966 he became a student which meant he could now afford private tuition, studying composition and techniques which involved changing from water-colours to oils. In order to compare his work with that of able-bodied students he became a member of a portrait class. Five years later his work earned him full membership and from then on he was financially independent and able to afford his own fees at Athol House.

In 1975 Paul married a girl from Switzerland and two years later the first of their two sons was born, the second arriving in 1979. The couple moved into a flat in a block specially built by the Greater London Council to be accessible for wheelchairs. A room in the flat overlooks a grassy garden with pleasant trees, and this is Paul's studio where he works practically every day. The walls are decorated with his paintings and there are piles of reference books so that he can check that the details of the old time ships he loves to paint are correct.

Paul works in a wheelchair from which the footrests have been removed. His easel is set at a tilted angle on a chair and an extra large palette is placed on the floor below. When it comes to mixing paint on it he does not need to have someone come and unscrew the caps from his paint tubes, he merely keeps uncapped tubes upside down in jars of water which prevents the oil paint from drying. From childhood Paul has been fascinated by ships – as a boy his greatest desire was to sail on a windjammer – and now that fascination is captured on his evocative marine canvases.

Charles Fowler

'The quality of acceptance'

When Charles Fowler was eighteen he had a dream in which he saw himself on a railway track covered in blood. Over the image of his dream appeared the words 'beware of Wednesday'. He was exceptionally careful alighting from the train on the Wednesday but on Thursday, being in a hurry to meet a friend, he opened the door of the railway carriage too quickly, slipped and fell between the platform and the line. The train wheels amputated his arms above the elbows.

'There is no doubt that I did dream my accident,' Charles says today. ' I have had many "foretelling" dreams since then, one example being when the husband of one of my friends died. I dreamt that he had a dark brown walking stick with a silver top. I telephoned my friend and described it to her and she said "Oh yes, there it is, by the side of his chair."'

Perhaps because of his unusual experiences there is an element of fatalism in his philosophical makeup.

Charles Fowler was born in Chelsea and had a very happy homelife in the London suburb of Wimbledon. His easy-going nature protected him against the problems which threaten some only children. He enjoyed school where his favourite subjects were geography, history and art, a subject in which he won several prizes which encouraged him to consider the possibility of getting a place in art school. In the end he yielded to practical considerations and sat for a London Chamber of Commerce examination. Having passed his exams, Charles was employed by a firm in Mincing Lane. A year later he had his accident and his career in London was at an end.

Charles was to remain in hospital for two months, during which time he attempted to come to terms with his new circumstances.

'It is a lifetime ago and I hardly ever think about it now,' he says today. 'But I remember I found it less difficult that you might imagine. It was a great nuisance of course, but the point was I was very young and therefore it was much more easy for me to adapt than if I had been twenty-five or thirty. And I was helped by the sheer sense of not worrying – I had the quality of acceptance, as indeed most disabled people have too.'

But if Charles was prepared to accept the fact that he had had both arms amputated, it did not mean that he was going to meekly accept the fact of his disability.

'I think one of the best things I ever did was to say to myself: "When I can leave hospital I'm not going to go home in a car, I'm going to walk back." And walk back he did to his parents' Wimbledon home.

It was after his return from hospital that Charles felt an urge to paint so he took to holding a brush in his mouth.

"There was no other way of doing it," he explains. "And even in the beginning I had very little difficulty with this method.

As I said, I was very adaptable then. And compared with so many mouth and foot artists, I am extremely lucky in that I do not have a breathing problem and I can walk.'

The subject for Charles' first attempt as a mouth painter was a tulip in a vase. Soon afterwards he painted a May tree in blossom. This proved to be a very popular picture with friends and acquaintances and so many offered to buy it that Charles set up a production line of May tree studies with seven paintings being worked on simultaneously. The fact that he could earn money from his art, even though it had been produced by a brush

CHARLES FOWLER   *The Road to la Coupée, Sark*   Oil   90 x 63 cm

CHARLES FOWLER *Winter Snow* Watercolour

CHARLES FOWLER *Autumn Landscape* Watercolour 37 x 55 cm

CHARLES FOWLER *West Wales* Oil

CHARLES FOWLER *Herm & Jethou, from Sark* Watercolour

Overleaf:
CHARLES
FOWLER
In the Park
Watercolour
37 x 55 cm

75

KRIS KIRK *Boats at Sea* Oil   40 x 34 cm

KRIS KIRK
Windmill
Oil   45 x 35 cm

KRIS KIRK   *By the Banks of the River*   Oil   41 x 51 cm

79

KRIS KIRK   *Boats at the Shore*   Oil   35 x 45 cm

KRIS KIRK
Fun on the Ice
Oil   30 x 40 cm

ALISON LAPPER
Waterlilies
Crayon   22 x 28 cm

ALISON LAPPER   *'Trees in Pink'* Crayon   23 x 27 cm

ALISON LAPPER *Composition* Watercolour 19 x 24 cm

BRUCE PEARDON   *On the Sea*   Watercolour   17 x 24 cm

BRUCE PEARDON   *End of Winter*   Watercolour   25 x 32 cm

BRUCE PEARDON   *Animal World*   Oil   46 x 61 cm

BRUCE PEARDON   *Fishing*   Watercolour   30 x 35 cm

BRUCE PEARDON *Grandfather, Koala & Possum;* an illustration from *Old Billy's children's book*

Overleaf: BRUCE PEARDON *Gores Farm, Surrey* Oil 37 x 51 cm

BRUCE PEARDON   *Concerto in Oils*   Oil   40 x 60 cm

BRUCE PEARDON   *Still Life with Globe*   Oil   31 x 51 cm

clamped between his teeth, was a great encouragement and Charles decided to develop his talent. To this end he began lessons in the studio of a professional artist in Tulse Hill, which meant a rail journey from Wimbledon. Despite his traumatic experience at Wimbledon Station, Charles was determined to go backwards and forwards alone, and developed a technique for opening carriage doors with his foot.

By this time he had artificial arms fitted at Queen Mary's Hospital, Roehampton, and found that these limbs greatly increased his independence. 'I am fortunate in being able to eat with a specially designed fork, to shave, to play chess and to perform other functions, besides possessing two useful defensive weapons!' he says.

It was then decided that Charles should attend an art school. 'I rather wondered how I would be received at my first class,' he says, 'but I found it to be much better than I expected. When I was sent to the life room I picked up a pencil in my teeth to start drawing and everybody looked round – and after that I was ignored as an oddity and accepted as a student who could draw.'

When Charles had attended art school for four years, he was awarded the Ministry of Education's Award of High Merit. After this he won an Exhibition Scholarship to the Royal College of Art where he studied for a further four years, taking a Continuation Scholarship and gaining his diploma. But when college life came to its conclusion, Charles had to think seriously about making a living out of art which is one of the hardest professions in which to get established. Although his work was exhibited in various galleries, including those of the Royal Academy, the Royal Society of British Artists, The London Group of Artists of Fame and Promise and the Royal Society of Painting in Water Colour, Charles wanted the security of a regular income.

The artist with whom he had had his first lessons at Tulse Hill was now the Principal of Farnham School of Art and, having followed Charles' progress over the years, now offered him the post of teaching Still Life one day a week.

When he introduced the new lecturer to his class, the principal told them 'not to be nervous with Mr. Fowler', adding that it would be a kindness if someone would light a cigarette for him if he needed it. Charles then began teaching, and half way through his work he asked a student to take a cigarette from the packet in his pocket and give him a light when he had got it between his lips. Feeling more relaxed Charles continued the lesson until the cigarette was burning uncomfortably close to his mouth. Without thinking he flicked it into a wastepaper basket with a jerk of his head. The class watched wide-eyed as the basket, which contained some turpentine-soaked waste, erupted with a gush of flame – a spectacular way of beginning a teaching career, Charles decided.

Apart from this conflagration he found that he enjoyed lecturing and would like to do more of it. He visited various art schools where he did his best to convince those in charge that his disability was no handicap when it came to imparting knowledge. as a result he was given work as an evening lecturer at Richmond Institute. This situation was ideal because it left him time for his own painting, and at the same time provided him with an absorbing interest as he came to realize how much teaching meant to him. And the fact that he had found his real vocation was proved a few years later when he was invited to become lecturer in charge of the Richmond Institute's art department, and then its head, a post which he held for the next fifteen years. During that time the number of students enrolled in his care rose from eight hundred to two thousand.

'I am lucky that I still have many friends from those days,' Charles says. ' I had a staff of four full-time lecturers and twenty part-timers, and I am still in touch with many of them.'

In 1963 Charles' mother died, followed by his father two years later, and he had to face the prospect of life on his own which can be very daunting for the disabled. What he really needed was someone to keep house for him and attend his needs, and he decided to go to the Citizens' Advice Bureau in the hope that they could put him in touch with someone suitable. By a happy coincidence a lady who had been recently widowed went to the same bureau the next day to say that, now she was on her own, she wanted to get involved in helping someone in need of assistance. The secretary of the Bureau introduced them and was gratified to see that they took to each other, and the outcome of the meeting was that Charles found an ideal person to keep house for him.

'I was so lucky to find her,' Charles says. 'She is one of the most unselfish and helpful people I have met.'

During college vacations Charles travelled extensively, and still does, particularly in remote and unspoilt spots which are reflected in his painting.

'I am an Atlantic rather than a Mediterranean person,' he explains. 'I love feeling the power of the wind and watching the movement of the sea.' One of his favourite places is Sark in the Channel Islands.

'If there's nobody around I like to paint on the spot,' he adds. 'It's strange that, after all this time, I get a little unsure when I know there are people about watching me. I know it's silly but I'm not like Erich Stegmann who couldn't care less who was watching him. I was lucky enough to meet him several times – what a wonderful man he was.'

Charles retired from college work in 1975, and it was then that a friend suggested that he should get in contact with the Association of Mouth and Foot Artists, an organisation of which he had not heard. Intrigued, he visited the Association's office where the work was explained to him which made him all the more interested in the Association, so much so that he submitted eight water colours. These were of such a high standard that he was given full membership immediately.

Apart from work, Charles continued to travel in order to get new subjects. He enjoys listening to music – Mozart always, but he is catholic in his musical tastes.

'I have many interests outside painting, chess being one of my time consuming hobbies and I enjoy the study of history, geography and ornithology. I like good food and wine and perhaps would have liked to cook.

'Although I am disabled, as far as possible I refuse to admit it and do not like the word, though it is difficult to find a satisfactory alternative. Handicapped people generally are subject to a great deal of misplaced sympathy. When this sympathy and help is understanding and unobtrusive it is welcomed gratefully. When it is sentimental and sensational it is not.

'But I remember, when travelling through France with a friend, how the words "sentimental" and "sensational" took on a different meaning. We stopped at a lovely hotel on the upper Seine, ate a very good dinner at the end of which the proprietor came to our table and asked how I lost my arms. Before I could reply, my friend stated to my horror, that I had been a Captain of tanks and had been blow up by a mine in Italy during the war.

"How very sad," said the patron.

"Not at all," I replied. "One has love, the beauty of nature, and there is always cognac."

'He promptly brought a bottle which he helped me to drink, eventually becoming sentimental and the result the next morning for me anyway was certainly sensational!'

During the 1988 MFPA Delegates' Conference held in London Charles was elected to the Board of the Association by unanimous vote and now travels to Liechtenstein twice yearly to attend Board meetings there with members from different parts of the world.

Kris Kirk

'I prefer to believe.'

Despite the fact that Kris Kirk has to spend his waking life in a wheelchair there is an aura of restless energy about him. The breadth of his shoulders still suggest the athlete and he paints with the same determination that as a youth he devoted to sport – once he almost made it into the England Junior Rugby Team.

In 1973 he enjoyed great success on the games field; at school he was captain of the cricket, baseball and rugby teams, and it was in the latter game that he represented London, Middlesex and South East England. All this ended abruptly when, during a family outing at Brighton, fifteen-year-old Kris dived off a groyne and his head struck the sandy bottom.

'When I came up to the surface I opened my eyes and found that I could not move,' he says. 'My body refused to obey me and I just floated.'

His cousin realized there was something wrong and brought him ashore where he lay on the beach unable to move. an ambulance was called and Kris was taken to Brighton Hospital where his family was told that his neck was broken. After two days in traction he was taken to Stoke Mandeville Hospital for specialized treatment which was to last for a year. Every effort was made by physiotherapists to bring back the use of his muscles but to no avail. When the specialists had to admit that he would never have control over his hands again, various gadgets were tried by which it was hoped he would be able to write by using the slight movement that was left in his arm.

Although ingenious, these devices were too complicated for Kris and he knew that if he used them he would always need someone to fit them to him. In the end it was decided to see if he could learn to write by the far less complicated method of holding a pencil in his mouth. In the occupational therapy department he began to practise the technique.

'They thought it would be useful if I could write letters,' Kris explains. 'At that time, even though I had taken an O-level in art, it did not occur to me that there was any future for me as an artist. But once when I was not busy practising the alphabet I did try a drawing. It was of a lion, but as to how good it was I can only say that when my doctor came on his rounds and saw it he quoted, "Tyger, Tyger burning bright ..."'

After Stoke Mandeville Kris returned to his family in London, and found it to be very supportive. Although he is English born, his parents came from Cyprus and they retained the strong Greek Cypriot sense of family. In order that he should continue his studies, lessons were brought to his home by teachers. One of these was an art teacher and when he saw the progress the disabled youth was making in the subject with a mouth-held pencil he arranged for him to go to college once a week. The result was that Kris got an A-level in art, and after this Rehab, a Government-backed organization, arranged for an art teacher to visit him regularly.

Kris was grateful for this help but now admits that the work he was expected to do was not very exciting.

'I was doing art but sometimes it would take me weeks to draw a potato on a plate,' he says.

Kris had several Rehab teachers, and it was the final one named Fred Bloomfield who had a tremendous effect on him.

'He's an incredible artist,' Kris says. 'He likes to paint surreal subjects best, and sometimes he'll work on a canvas for a year until it's perfect . He was – and still is – a real friend. He gave me loads of technical advice, and even suggested that someday I might make a living out of painting.'

In 1978 Kris remembered that a physiotherapist had once told him about the Mouth and Foot Painting Artists and now he decided to approach the Association. In response to his letter Kris was visited by Charles Fowler who looked carefully through his paintings, selecting some to take away for the Association to assess.

'Then at Christmas I received word from the Association and it was the best Christmas present I ever had,' says Kris. 'They were willing to take me on as a student which meant that I would be helped financially. and for me the great thing was that I would be able to work at home.'

At that time much of Kris's work was surrealistic reflecting the influence of his teacher Fred Bloomfield, and now that he had been accepted as a student he knew he would have to tackle other forms of painting.

'After all, you can't have surreal calendar and Christmas card illustrations,' he says. The thing that mattered most in his life was to improve his painting so that he would be accepted as a member of the Association. To this end he started work each morning at ten o'clock with his palette and paints laid out in front of his easel and a brush held firmly in his teeth, and, with only a break of half an hour, he would paint on until seven at night when he was usually so fatigued he could not do any more. Such a regime made him one of the most prolific mouth painters and every three months he submitted on average sixteen of his best paintings. His hard work paid off in 1982 when he achieved his ambition of full membership.

'That was the best thing that has happened to me since my accident,' he says. 'The Association is so caring. I often suffer with kidney infections as a result of being immobilized and while I am being treated for it I find it impossible to paint, yet I am not made to feel that I am letting them down.'

Becoming a member gave Kris financial security and enabled him to afford to make a pilgramage to the island he had heard so much about since childhood – Cyprus, the home of his forebears whose name was Kyriacou. He did not fly there as he decided that travelling overland with his family across Europe in his own transport would give him freedom to travel about the island (or at least the Greek section) when they arrived.

Kris recalls, 'The bad part of the journey was before we actually set off – there was so much to think of. My special mattresses had to be taken with us as well as a lot of medical equipment. But once we were on our way I felt fine, and rather than have the problems which might arise with me staying at strange hotels, we camped out which added to the fun. We spent nights in Belgium, Germany, Yugoslavia and Greece. Then we had a two-day voyage to Cyprus where we stayed for six weeks. It was the first time I had ever visited the place where my Mum and Dad came from and I met my relatives for the first time. It was great – and upsetting, and the experience of a lifetime.'

In talking to the author, Kris described how he was taken to a monastery where he found a number of monks in heavy black robes sitting outside and patiently painting icons. Suffering from the heat himself, he wondered how these religious artists managed to stay cool enough to paint in their stifling clothes but he did not stay long enough to find the answer.

The monks had an apiary nearby and the number of bees hovering around the wheelchair 'frightened the living daylights' out of Kris. He tells it as an amusing anecdote but it does underline the plight of the paralysed. For the able-bodied the wave of a hand is usually good enough protection against flies, mosquitoes and wasps, but a person like Kris has no personal defence against the insect world and this can be a problem not only to him but all disabled artists who like to paint out of doors.

Cyprus made such an impact on Kris that he has now made his home there though he makes frequent visits to England. For this he is grateful to the Mouth and Foot Painting Artists.

'If you are disabled like me you have to make money to get what you need, and the Association enables you to do this,' he explains. 'If I had not been working for them I would never have been able to go to Cyprus in the first place. It offers more than a job – it's like a social service. Ordinary people do not worry how they are going out for a walk or maybe visit a beach, but if you are paralysed and you haven't got a van, and if you haven't got a wheelchair fitted so that you can control it yourself, you have to stay at home all the time.'

Like many other disabled people Kris gets a lot of comfort and companionship from his pet – in his case a Doberman Pinscher named Czar who has been with him since he was a pup. Before his accident he had Lad, a Collie who he still misses.

'When Lad died at the age of fourteen I had never felt so devastated,' Kris says. 'People might think it's silly to have been so upset over an animal but he was special. Lad was closer to me than Czar can be because he could remember how I used to romp with him before my accident, which is something I can never do with Czar. When I was in Stoke Mandeville Lad was brought to see me in the grounds of the hospital. I hadn't seen him for a long time but he ran over to me and there was great joy between us.

'He had gotten lost while I was away, and then he was found at the Battersea Dogs' Home. He had caught a disease that nearly killed him but when the vet wanted to put him down my Mum wouldn't let him because she knew what Lad meant to me and she managed to nurse him through. When he was better he was brought to see me and I vividly remember how cracked the skin of his nose was – funny the little things that come back to you.'

Today Kris continues to work as hard as ever though at times he has to leave off to go to hospital – on average he spends three months a year there with medical problems – and he usually completes a painting once a fortnight. He works in oils with short-handled brushes which give him more control of the paint though this does strain his eyesight through working with his face close to the canvas.

'I put my paintings straight on to the canvas after drawing the outlines in paint – not pencil – and in my mind I know exactly what I want to do,' he explains. 'I like very controlled, tight paintings. Every speck of paint I put down I put there deliberately – not because the brush happened to hit there.'

Speaking of the effect disability has had on his life Kris says that if his accident had not happened he would probably have got married – and then adds, 'But a lot of people who are married regret it, so it's hard to say...

'What I do regret is not being able to play sport, especially as a lot of my friends who I went to school with still take part in it. For me Rugby was not just a game, it was a way of life at the Christopher Wren School I went to. The head boy was always a Rugby player and this was nearly always the case with prefects. You got privileges if you were good at Rugby and you got on better with the teachers. Although it was a London comprehensive it was Rugby mad and I loved it.'

'I find it's best not to dwell on the past, if you thought about it too much you'd go crazy. I just concentrate on the things that I am good at today and keep them to the forefront. I can't play Rugby any more but I play a lot of chess – sometimes by telephone with Charles Fowler. And I can give my computer a good game.

'I like to think there is some magic in the world. I'd like to think that unicorns once existed ... And it's the same with religion, I prefer to believe. No one can say definitely whether there is a God or life after death, but those who do believe do have the consolation and uplift of their faith through life and if they are wrong and there is nothing it does not matter because they will never know ...

'But I must admit that there have been times when I thought God has been unfair but then how can one expect life to be perfect? I think I am unlucky compared with many people and very lucky compared with a lot of others. People often say it but it is true, there is always someone worse off than you. And I think of this when I see famine pictures from Africa, and when I've encountered dossers down the road and have seen drug addicts whose minds are completely gone, I wonder what the hell I'm complaining about.'

Alison Lapper

'Hopefully you enjoy me as I am'

'Idid not realize I was disabled until I was thirteen – can you believe that! ' Alison Lapper declares with a characteristic laugh. To the able-bodied such a statement sounds far-fetched yet if one had grown to that age in an institution surrounded by a hundred other disabled children it is understandable. It also suggests that up until then there was no trauma for Alison because disability was the norm. The trauma came with the sudden understanding that in the world outside there were tall people with fully developed limbs who could run and dance and enjoy themselves in whatever way they wished and to whom pain was a rare annoyance easily assuaged.

'The realization came when I went to a "normal" youth club,' Alison recalls. 'It was a terrible shock. I wanted to kill myself. It was the most crucial time in my life. I had just had a major operation – they took out my ankle bone and turned my foot right round. I was starting to get interested in boys while this was going on and I did not know what to do with myself. I felt I was going backwards rather than forward. You realize that your able-bodied friends are going to get boyfriends and you are not. It took me until I was sixteen to come to terms with my disability.'

Today she had more than come to terms with it, pursuing a life and career with a zest that the able-bodied might envy. But behind her easy confidence is a story of a very hard won victory.

At first sight people take Alison for a victim of thalidomide but with a flash of her quirky humour she explains, 'I'm just a natural abnormality.' She does not use the correct name for her complaint because she cannot remember how to spell it but it is phocomela.

Alison was born in 1965 in Burton-on-Trent and as a result of phocomelia she arrived in the world with arms and legs that were no more than tiny stumps. Her mother was told with that amazing lack of tact one sometimes encounters in 'straight-from-the-shoulder-no-nonsense' medical people that if the infant survived she would never be more than a 'stuffed cabbage in a wheelchair'. It was too much for the shocked woman who left the hospital without even seeing her baby daughter.

When this limbless scrap of humanity had survived for five weeks she was taken to the Chailey Heritage, a centre for the young disabled and which was to be her home for the next seventeen years.

'Part hospital, part school, it was a little world of its own,' Alison told the author. 'At first I was in the hospital section looked after by nurses and as I grew older I progressed through different wards. I was mostly with thalidomides and there were a lot of experiments done with artificial limbs. At times we were like guinea-pigs.'

'I did not see my parents until I was four and after that I stayed with them during school holidays but my real home was Chailey and it was really good for someone like me. The staff pushed you the whole time. The message was always, "You must be independent – you must do it on your own."

'Chailey was my life, and I used to think "What am I going to do when I leave here?" When the time came to go I was so petrified at the thought of leaving that I refused to budge. It took four people to put me on the coach.'

From Chailey Alison went to the Banstead Place Residential Centre in Surrey.

'At Chailey I had been considered a slow learner but at Banstead they really gave me a big kick up the backside – "Come on, pull your socks up, girl!"'

To get her integrated with the outside world the staff sent Alison down to the village to collect her own money and look after herself. Everything was new to her. Up until then she did not know what a cheque was. Wearing artificial legs, she was sent to a normal school nearby where by using a mouthstick she found a lot of pleasure in drawing. Her first efforts were little matchstick figures, pages and pages of them which like a comic strip played out stories running through her head – usually tragic love affairs.

At school she passed her CSE's and at this time entered a contest that was to change her life. It was a school painting competition with a trip to Lourdes as the first prize. Alison, now graduated from her Lowry-like stick figures, painted a scene showing one of the Stations of the Cross. To her delighted amazement it was announced that she had won and a newspaper carried an article about the disabled girl who painted with a brush held in her mouth.

As with other artists mentioned in this book, the Association of Mouth and Foot Painting Artists picked up the story and after her work had been evaluated she was offered a scholarship.

When she was nineteen Alison insisted on coming up to London. The Banstead Centre accepted her determination to leave and found her a room in a hostel in Baron's Court. From here she attended the West London College to do an A-Level in art.

'I failed miserably,' she admits, 'but in other ways college was a success. It made me force myself to get over my fear of people. The college was massive – and rather rough – and I found everything hard because I felt there was something incredibly wrong about me. To try and look more normal I used to wear my artificial legs.'

The Association assumed more and more importance in her life and after she finished at the West London College arrangements were made for her to attend the Heatherly School of Fine Art situated off New King's Road. In order to go there from the ground floor flat she happily occupied alone in a quiet street in Hammersmith, the Association helped her to acquire a specially adapted Mini Metro in which she passed her driving test the first time.

Another ambition Alison fulfilled was to learn to ride a horse. To do this she attended a riding school in Wormwood Scrubs where, holding the reins in her teeth, she joined able-bodied riders.

Alison has come a long way from the frightened girl who had to be forced on to the coach leaving Chailey and without doubt the key to her independence is her enthusiasm for art. Few able-bodied artists can have the same exuberant love for their subject. Thanks to a portfolio of her work which she built up while at the Heatherly School of Fine Arts she was accepted in 1990 by the Brighton Polythechnic for a degree course.

Alison approaches art with the same gutsy confidence as she approaches life.

'When it comes to materials I have tried everything,' she says. 'I nearly poisoned myself with oils. Now I use gouache and water-colour. But I believe texture is equally important as the colours you use and I have painted on everything from calico to tissue paper to get effects I want. In fact I paint on anything I can get hold of that has an interesting texture. Sometimes I build up the picture with Polyfilla to achieve a dimensional appearance.

'My paintings are mostly about people and how I integrate with them; how other people affect me and how I affect them and how I feel about life deep down. I love life classes and I love to paint beautiful bodies. You might think it is some sort of wishful thinking, that I am portraying how I think I ought to be but it's not a negative thing. It is not me saying "This is how I wish I was." This is me saying "I look at your body and find it beautiful." To capture the beauty of the human body is what I strive for all the time. I suppose I am saying "I know I am like I am but I can enjoy you as you are, and hopefully you can enjoy me as I am." '

Some time ago Alison gave up using her artificial legs.

'I used to wear them to try and look normal – I felt I ought to be 5' 1", she explains. 'Then as I got older I thought, "Who am I trying to kid?" I don't need to have arms and legs if I can come cross as a reasonable human being.

'I felt a great sense of achievement when I decided to do this and get about on the stumps I had – I have even been to nightclubs without my "legs". And the more people who meet me as I am the more people will be comfortable with disabled persons.

'When people make a mistake and go to shake hands with me or hand me a cup of tea, it is not an embarrassment but the biggest compliment I could have above everything else because they forget I am disabled and just see me as Alison.'

Bruce Peardon

Bushland Inspiration

*I*t is a warm summer evening in the Australian countryside. In an old fashioned horse-drawn *cart a farmer, his wife and their small son are returning howeward from town. The little boy is so tired from the excitement of the expedition that he lies sleeping in the back of the cart with his teddy bear. When they are nearly home the cart lurches and unnoticed Teddy falls on to the dirt road.*

On reaching home the farmer carries the sleeping child straight to bed and it is not until next morning that he becomes aware of his loss. Meanwhile Teddy spends the night on the road but with the sunrise various indigenous Australian animals gather to help him, a wombat, possum, emu, kangeroo and other bushland creatures ...

The above is the opening scenes of a children's book told in verse entitled *Teddy's Night Lost in the Bush* and much of its delight comes from its lovingly painted illustrations depicting the bush animals. Ever since Theodore Roosevelt inspired the manufacture of teddy bears they have proved to be winners in children's fiction – one only has to think of Pooh, Paddington and Rupert! Here a teddy bear succeeds yet again, this time as the character who introduces young Australian children to their wildlife heritage though the appeal of the book has spread far beyond Australian shores and is now published in Sweden.

The book by Bruce Peardon, published by the Association of Mouth and Foot Painting Artists, follows the success of his first children's book *Charlie the Chimneysweep and Sooty* which was a Victorian Christmas story.

Bruce dedicated his teddy bear book to his son Ben 'in the fervent hope that his and future generations will have the opportunity to enjoy the unique fauna and flora of his homeland, Australia.'

Bruce's latest book *Old Billy's Enchanted Valley*, again beautifully illustrated by pictures of Australian wildlife, has an environmental theme as can be appreciated through the words of an old kangaroo talking to his grandson, 'We are all creatures on this earth and we have to share ... but they are slowly learning that every living thing on earth is here for a purpose and if they interfere with the wonders of Nature too much, then they will lose it all.'

The book also bravely introduces the idea of death into the story when Grandpa Kangaroo explains that Old Billy, a man who replanted a deforested valley, had died with the words '... like all creatures when they become very sick or old, Old Billy died. So his friends in the valley put him in the ground and put a stone where he lies ... all of us die when we are old ... our bodies may go away but all of us keep living by the memories we leave with others.'

Bruce and his wife Christine built their house in a woodland inspiring his paintings of bush scenes and the enigmatic landscapes of Australia – his other favourite subject being children in amusing situations which has proved particularly popular on greeting cards produced by the Association.

Bruce was seventeen when he was involved in an accident that left him a quadriplegic. Two years earlier he had joined the Australian Navy as a junior recruit and after initial training at Perth was transferred to Flinders Naval Depot in Victoria. In October 1962 he and a friend went on leave together. The return journey to base was a long one and meant driving through the night. Bruce drove until fatigue overtook him and then his companion took the wheel while he went to sleep across the back seat. The next thing he was aware of was lying in a hospital bed, having no recollection of his friend dozing off, the car going out of control and the crash in which his spine was injured.

Things did not seem too bad for the first three weeks in hospital, then he had a relapse and with it came the realization that he would be paralysed for the rest of his life. As is seen by the stories of the artists in this book, each person has his or her way of coming to terms with disability. Bruce says that for the first quarter of an hour he was devastated when it was broken to him that he would not get the use of his limbs back, 'but after that I just concentrated on getting on with life. I was lucky that I was young and young people are adaptable.'

His adaptability was proved when in Melbourne's Austin Hospital he saw two patients hard at work painting with brushes held in their mouths. Bill Mooney and the late James Meath were members of the Association of Mouth and Foot Painting Artists.

'The way they painted inspired me to do the same,' Bruce recalls. 'I had painted for a hobby and strangely enough to paint with a brush held between my teeth – apart from the problem of biting the end off from time to time – seemed a perfectly natural way to paint right from the start. We are all part of the animal kingdom and animals have a knack of adapting very quickly to changes in their condition, and so it was for me. When I could no longer use my hands I found I could write almost immediately with a pencil held between my teeth, so when it came to painting I had no difficulty in using a brush this way. It was learning the correct techniques of painting that I had to concentrate on.'

One odd thing that he found was that being left-handed he paints with the brush held in the left side of his mouth.

For the next two years he persevered at his easel and studied the effect of colours upon each other, perspective and composition until he felt confident enough to follow the example of the other two mouth-painters and apply to the Association to become a student. His hard work was rewarded when the samples he submitted were judged to be of a high enough standard for his application to be accepted.

Soon after he was enjoying the benefits of being a student a big change took place in Bruce's life. No matter how well a severely disabled person is cared for in hospital he or she tends to become institutionalized, and Bruce and some other disabled people in the hospital wanted to prove that they could live outside hospital and by doing so it would be cheaper for the Social Services to maintain them. They acquired a house and set up their own community which, while not unique in Australia today, was a brave pioneering project in the 'sixties.

It was lack of funds which ended the experiment but it had given Bruce a taste of independence and he had no wish to go back to an institutional life. Helped by his income from the Association he managed to get a house of his own where he arranged for a young married couple to look after him in return for accommodation. Here he spent his time working to improve his painting as full membership of the Association was now his goal. He found it impossible to attend ordinary art classes so he worked on a programme of self-instruction in which he toured galleries to familiarize himself with the work of well-known artists, and studied art books to analyse the techniques of classic painters.

During this time he evolved his own philosophy of art, saying, 'I think there is too much pretentiousness in the art world – people think one has to be a Van Gogh, or starve to death in a garret. I believe one has to paint to live, and therefore I look upon myself as a commercial painter in that if I am commissioned to do a landscape or a portrait that is exactly what I have to do.'

In 1970, after Bruce had been working as a student for six years, his goal was achieved and he was made a full member of the Association, and soon afterwards held several one-man exhibitions of his work. It was a good year, but what capped it was his meeting with a nurse named Christine Halliday whom he married in 1973. Four years later they were able to buy a piece of land set in Bruce's beloved bushland seventeen miles south-west of Brisbane and here they had their house built.

'It's very conducive to painting,' says Bruce, 'being surrounded by lovely trees and plenty of animal and bird life.' The latter no doubt provided inspiration for *Teddy's Night Lost in the Bush.*

In 1983 Benjamin was born to Christine and Bruce who felt more frustration than he had ever experienced in twenty years of being disabled at not being able to pick up his son. He suffered an ache at not being able to give him a hug if he fell over or lift him on to his knee to tell him stories, but this passed with time and Benjamin learning to walk so that he could race to Bruce's wheelchair if he was in trouble. Before long he understood that his Dad could not do things like him and he began to help Bruce by fetching things for him and even helping him to adjust his easel. This seemed so natural to the boy that when he began drawing for the first time he held the pencil in his mouth.

Bruce's child studies which have proved so popular are mostly modelled on Benjamin. Boys are too lively to hold poses so his mother shoots rolls of film of him to freeze a gesture or a passing smile for Bruce to paint. For such paintings, which are used for cards, Bruce uses gouache because of its opaque colour effect, but for his landscapes he prefers to work in oils.

Sometimes it seems to Bruce there is not enough time for him to do all the things he wants to. Apart from his regular painting, he visits schools to demonstrate mouth painting as part of his talks on the subject of disability and he also takes a great – and much appreciated – interest in his fellow mouth-painting artists.

With Christine he makes long journeys about the continent in order to find landscapes which she will photograph for future reference.

Since being elected to the international board of the AMFPA he visits Europe twice a year to represent his fellow Australasian artists at the Association's regular meetings.

When he is not painting in his bushland home he likes to relax by watching sport – Rugby Union and cricket in particular – on television or listening to music which ranges from Australian folk songs.to Beethoven. One of his great pleasures is to coach one of the local school's Rugby teams from his wheelchair.

Edward Rainey

'If you don't try you've failed.'

'I was as fit as a fiddle and that's what saved me,' explains Edward Rainey when discussing the accident that left his body and limbs without movement. 'And I have the army to thank for that. Service life gives you an attitude that sustains you regardless of what happens.'

If it was his military background that supported him during the days he was poised between life and death, he has no doubt that it was a spiritual reawakening that enabled him to face the years that followed.

In his Glasgow home, where the walls are adorned with his paintings, he described to the author the background of events that led up to a mystical transformation of his life.

'I had an ordinary happy childhood with my younger brother and older sister at our home in Pollok,' he said. 'I was baptised a Roman Catholic but I became non-practising – I just enjoyed living life as it came. After leaving school I worked in a butcher's until one day I felt there was more to life than working inside all the time. So I joined the Royal Highland Fusiliers because I wanted adventure – and I certainly got it. I did abseiling, parachuting, jumping from helicopters, a skiing instructor's course... and I served for five-and-a-half months in Northern Ireland which was an experience in itself.

'Then, when I was twenty-four I went to Spain for a holiday with my friend Eddie – we were known as "the two Eddies" – and as soon as we arrived at our hotel in Marbella we decided to have a swim in the pool. I dived into the shallow end by mistake and struck my head on the bottom. In that moment I lost all control of my body, I was just drifting about underwater but I had enough presence of mind to hold my breath until someone realized what had happened and got me out.'

Eddie was flown back to Scotland by air ambulance and in hospital his mother and father were told that he had no more than three days to live – his spinal cord had been severed when his head struck the bottom of the pool. He was given the last rites, but the young patient who had been in peak physical condition clung to life and confounded the medical experts.

'I had been so physically active that I found the immobilisation hard to cope with,' Eddie said. 'I was so depressed that I cried an ocean at the beginning. I kept asking "Why me?" but later I answered myself with "Why not me?"

'I remember being put in a wheelchair and parked alone for hours and hours in front of a window looking down on a carpark when what I really wanted was someone to talk to. Sometimes a book was put in front of me but a book isn't much use if you can't turn the pages. Looking back on that time I don't know how I came through – but what I do know is that I did not come through it by myself. It was as though there was somebody pulling me through the shadows.'

After months of specialized treatment Eddie was allowed to return to his parents' home and a wheelchair-bound future. As the flat was on the fourth floor of a tenement it was so difficult for him to be taken downstairs that he hardly ever went out.

'I felt I had to do something other than stare out of the window or watch television,' Eddie continued. 'I desperately needed something positive in my life and then – just at the right time – my aunt brought me a calendar from the Mouth and Foot Painting Artists' Association. Looking at it I felt inspired to try painting myself and I began my mouth-painting career by making charcoal sketches. When I was able to control a brush I went on to oil paints and for a while I tried putting on the colours with a palette knife but this turned out to be too difficult.

'Once I started painting I found there was not enough time in the day – life to me seems so very, very short. After four years I believed that I had reached a good enough standard to submit my work to the Association and as a result I became a student – so far the only one in Scotland.

'Apart from the feeling of achievement that this gave me it meant that through my painting I can support myself and don't have to depend on the State to look after me. My next goal is to become a full member, not just from the financial aspect but as an honour not only for myself but those around me. An accident like mine affects everybody, your family suffers as much as you do so it is a wonderful thing when they can share something good with you. You have to have such targets to strive for and I believe that if you don't try you've failed.'

Today Eddie works on his canvases as hard as ever despite the fact that he has considerable continuous pain in the back of his neck and left shoulder. Whenever possible he paints out of doors, going to country locations for his landscapes in the summer and painting scenes of his native city even in winter. [When the author interviewed him in December he was planning a night-painting expedition in George's Square so that he could capture the effect of the Christmas lights.]

Eddie has no inhibitions about painting publicly, on the contrary he enjoys chatting to the people who inevitably crowd round to watch his unusual style of painting.

'I love meeting people when I at work outdoors,' he says. 'All sorts come up to me, all nationalities, and many ask if they can take photographs of me at my easel. I don't mind – it's good when people who may buy our cards see a mouth or foot artist in action so they can appreciate what actually lies behind them.'

Eddie now lives at ground level in a house close to his parents which enables him to be looked after by his mother Cathy who he affectionately calls 'my wee ma.' He has a great many loyal friends and often in the evening goes out with them in his wheelchair for a drink at his local pub – being religious in no way inhibits his enjoyment of life.

Talking about his belief, Eddie says, 'God helps you through your life every day even if you don't want to believe it. It was about six years ago that I started to realize this. I was experiencing an overwhelming sensation of joy and love. I didn't know what it was but it kept getting stronger. At first I was afraid to tell my family because I didn't really know what it was myself, but I told them when I eventually realized that it was the presence of God that inspired these feelings.

'I now go to Mass and find that the spiritual comfort that comes with the Communion helps to me to keep on at what I am doing.

'At times I enjoy a wonderful sense of peace and I am happier than I was before the accident – it has made me a better person spiritually. Life is one big mystery but I feel that there is something within me that no earthly thing can touch, and that goodness never dies in people but moves on.'

Heather Strudwick

Sleeping now perhaps she dreams of home? All pink and lace her
bungalow. The dog waits by the door; bright colours smile from
paintings done-by-mouth. Undaunted spirit evident all round
despite the batteries, the pumps and iron-lung whose long-jawed
gape awaits the leavings of each day and tea-time's end.

Into her dreaming head I breathe a prayer for safe deliverance
back here to us who share the cares and caring of her world.
Goodnight my dear, brave sister – and sweet dreams!

The above lines are the last two verses of a poem entitled Dreams Are Now For Crying In... which was written by Patricia Crittenden about her sister Heather Strudwick who every night has to sleep in an iron lung as a result of poliomyelitis. In 1991 the poem won a national poetry competition sponsored by 'Crossroads' – a national caring organisation – and Patricia was invited to No 10 Downing Street to receive her prize from Mrs Norma Major.

As the poem was concerned with Heather she was also invited to attend the ceremony, and later she told the author with her usual humour, 'It was an exciting and interesting day, Mrs Major is a very charming lady. I was carried up four flights of stairs by four policemen, and on the way down we managed to knock three prime ministers off the wall! I haven't been invited back...'

The meeting with the poet and the artist was later featured in Norma Major's biography *Norma*, which is not surprising as the subject of the prize-winning poem is a very remarkable lady.

Heather was born in 1933 in Gibraltar where her father was a Lance Corporal in the British army. When she grew up in England she trained to become an orthopaedic nurse in Oxford where she fell in love with a young man whom she married when he completed his National Service and joined the police force. They set up home in Colchester where their son Paul was born and where Heather later took a job in a factory as an industrial nurse.

Up to this point the story had been a happy one, then in 1957 Heather became the victim of poliomyelitis. So badly paralysed that she could not breathe, she was sent to the Rush Green Hospital in Romford, the respiratory centre for Essex, where she was lifted into an iron lung. Apart from having to come to terms with the fact that she had changed overnight from a young woman full of energy to a dangerously ill patient, she was desperately anxious over the effect her illness would have on her husband and her baby son Paul then aged one year eight months.

After six weeks she was allowed to see him through a window, the risk of infection being too great to allow him to come closer. Only her head protruded from the collar of the massive machine on which she depended for life, and it was heartbreaking when he failed to recognize his mummy through the glass. This made Heather realize the hopelessness of her situation and it was a relief when her sister-in-law Sheila offered to take care of Paul. At first Heather's husband visited her regularly, then the time between his visits lengthened and often he did not turn up when he had promised. And as though this uncertainty was not enough, it was found that Heather was pregnant and was given the agonizing choice of whether or not she should be operated on. In the end she agreed it would be best to have the operation and when it was all over the doctor told her that they had found that the baby was dead.

Worried by the effect the lack of visits by her husband was having on Heather, the hospital authorities contacted the police station to which he was attached. It was suggested to his superior that he should be given special leave to visit his wife who was so seriously ill.

'But he has been given leave – and cash to cover his travelling expenses,' came surprised response.

The truth emerged that Heather's husband had found someone else and the 'expenses' had been used to entertain her.

The final blow came when Heather's sister-in-law wrote to her that if she was going to continue to look after little Paul she must be allowed to adopt him legally. 'We don't want to love Paul and then lose him, but if you will agree to us legally adopting him then you will make us all happy,' she said.

More than anything else this letter made Heather realize that she was disabled for life. She would never be able to do anything for her son and so she had to agree to the proposal.

Heather was to remain imprisoned in the iron lung for two years after which she learned 'frog breathing' in which the patient uses her tongue and throat muscles to replace the paralysed diaphragm for inducing air into her lungs. Although the technique was difficult to master, it meant that Heather was able to stay out of the iron lung for longer and longer periods, and though the only activity of which she was capable was a limited movement of her neck, she was able to sit up in a wheelchair. Wearing a Thompson Pneumabelt portable respirator, she learned to operate an electric typewriter using a mouthstick.

When she had been in hospital for eight years a friend gave Heather a copy of the book *God's Second Door* by J.H.Roesler which told the stories of a number of disabled artists who painted by holding brushes either in their mouths or by their toes.

Not dreaming that one day she would be included in a book on such artists herself, Heather was adamant that it would be impossible for her to do anything like that. But not wishing to disappoint her friend she did try, and to her surprise – despite the fact that paint ran in all directions – she rather enjoyed the attempt. She kept on trying and as time went by she became so proficient people actually began asking her for her paintings.

In 1964 Heather contacted the Association of Mouth and Foot Painting Artists which she had learned about through *God's Second Door*. The result was that after her work had been evaluated she was given a scholarship to enable to take her painting further.

The following year Heather fell in love. A widower named Ron Strudwick had taken a job as a hospital porter in order to be able to live in Colchester with his daughter. Remembering what became the happiest period of her life, Heather says, 'He used to lift me out of bed into my wheelchair. Soon he began to look in and say hello when he was passing. And at lunch time he would bring his sandwiches and sit beside me when I was painting outside in my wheelchair. He would squeeze out fresh paint or adjust the canvas on my easel and chat to me in the most entertaining way. I soon realized that he had an intuitive understanding, but one day I felt it necessary to ask him why he spent so much time with me. Was it out of pity? That was something I had to know.'

Ron replied that he enjoyed Heather's company – pity was something that had not occurred to him.

'Then he asked me to go out with him – just as if I were a normal person,' says Heather. 'It was rather nice and he took me to Felixstowe in his car for the afternoon. As we became increasingly fond of each other we decided that our friendship must progress or be knocked rather smartly on the head, so we consulted the doctor who told Ron that I might live for two days or twenty years. Then he wished us the best of luck.'

Ron and Heather were married and moved into a bungalow which, after a decade of hospital life, seemed like an impossible dream come true.

'Looking back on the way my first marriage had ended, I could hardly believe how fortunate I was to experience real love after being paralysed for so long,' Heather says. 'Ron was a very special person, completely selfless and though he was older than me it made no more difference to our relationship than my disability. We just lived for each other and used to joke that we were two old fogies, but in fact we were so happy we didn't need anything else.'

During this happy time Heather continued with her painting, trying different mediums until she found that oil paints suited her best. Full membership of the AMFPA was what she strove for.

After five years of 'the best marriage possible' Ron died and Heather was left to cope with both grief and the renewed problem of her disability. The authorities decided it would be best for her if she returned to hospital but thanks to her father coming to stay with her she managed to remain in her bungalow for a trial period of six months. The time ran out but she fought on for her independence.

When Heather needed a hip operation she was sent to St Thomas' Hospital in London which had assumed responsibility for all the respiratory cases in the country as they were few in number and it was thought it would be best for them to be under one central authority. By a stroke of luck the hospital was running an experimental project to find out if it was less expensive to keep patients in their own homes rather than hospitalized. The hip operation brought Heather to the notice of the medical authorities and she was included in the project which meant that she would have the benefit of paid residential help.

In March 1982 she had one of the best days in her life when she wrote to the Social Security authorities to inform them that she no longer required assistance as she had become financially independent – she had been accepted as a full member of the Association.

'It was the best letter I have ever written thanks to the Mouth and Foot Painting Artists,' she told the author emphatically. 'It is only because of the Association that I was able to buy my house and because of their continued support I have been able to add a garage, a conservatory and purchase an almost new car. As a result my life has expanded as I can travel in much more comfort.'

The other good thing to happen was the renewal of her relationship with her son, now grown up with his own business.

'My sister-in-law Sheila has been wonderful over Paul,' Heather declares. 'She has shared him with me and when he was at school she used to ring up to read out his reports and things like that. It has been a delicate situation but I am happy to say we never fell out. Now Paul comes to visit me with his wife and their two children.'

Today Heather is looked after by two helpers, each staying with her for three-and-a-half days a week. During the day she uses a portable respirator fitted to her wheelchair while at night she sleeps in a conventional iron lung.

'Looking back on my life I think I am awfully lucky because I have done everything – I do know what it is like to swim, to run, to dance and to ride,' Heather says. 'I had a normal marriage and a baby and later, after I got polio, I was lucky to have another very special marriage. People who are born disabled or who are disabled very young have not had the chances I have had. Some say that by being disabled later on you have more to miss but I don't see it that way. I like to feel that I know what it's like, and then I have to shut the door on regrets and just carry on.'

Heather's enthusiasm for art remains as keen as ever.

'When I start painting I know roughly the colours I shall need and a helper puts them out in blobs so that I can mix them myself,' she explains. 'The difficult part is keeping the colours constant because I paint in bits and occasionally upside down as I cannot reach across the whole canvas. It take me three weeks to a month to complete a picture, depending how quickly it dries. You can't paint on top of wet paint so usually I have three on the go at once.'

In July 1990 Heather arranged a remarkable garden party with a pig roast and buffet for a hundred-and-thirty people. It was to celebrate her thirty-third year of 'breathless happiness'!

John Savage

'Life doesn't end with a broken neck.'

A fierce wind filled the sails of the galleon so that she heeled dangerously as she raced over the foaming sea. Pennants streamed from her masthead, you could almost hear the thrumming of her rigging and incongruously on her high gilded stern was the name *Floss*.

As John Savage gazed at the first picture he had painted he was unaware that it marked a turning point in his life. At that moment his satisfaction lay in the fact that he had produced something through which he could express his thanks for support received at a period when he had every reason to feel embittered. In three years he had known despair and just when it seemed that he had got on top of his problems fate had dealt him a final blow. But whatever his feelings were over this, he counted himself lucky in having caring people about him and he was eager to show his appreciation, in this case to a nurse named Floss for whom the picture had been painted.

One of a family of thirteen, John Savage was born in Birmingham. Apart from woodwork and drawing classes he did not enjoy his schooldays and from time to time played truant. On leaving school he went into an engineering factory but after fifteen months the feeling of being 'shut in' became too claustrophobic and he went into railway wagon repair which suited him much better. After two years of National Service he returned to his work, married, settled down in Vauxhall, Birmingham, and became the father of three children.

So far it was what might have been termed an everyday story of a Birmingham lad, then his marriage broke up and his everyday world was shattered.

His unhappiness was compounded by the problem of caring for his children and 'at his wits' end' he moved to Somerset where he and the children stayed with his sister and brother-in-law with whom he worked in his building business.

It was while he was still emotionally stunned that through his sister he met a married couple named Frank and Brenda Cossey who befriended him.

Talking about that time Brenda remembers that John was so troubled he did not want to have anything to do with women. And John swears that it was the understanding of Frank and Brenda that 'got me going again.' He frequently visited their home and helped Frank in his work as a pig farmer. Gradually his former good spirits returned.

After two years in Somerset he decided that the time had come to return to Birmingham and set up a new home for the children. One weekend he took them to stay with their grandmother and then returned to finish the last job on which he was working with his brother-in-law. Although he would miss Somerset and his good friends the thought of the new life that lay ahead filled him with elation.

Early on a wintry Monday morning in 1965 the two men set off for Gwent for their final day's work on some new bungalows. At a crossroads a car shot out in front of them, the driver lost control on the icy road and crashed into their vehicle. When John was taken from the wreck it was found that his neck was broken.

'As a result of the accident I was in hospital for nine months – four of which I was in traction – while part of the time I was in the Stoke Mandeville Hospital,' John recalls. 'When I came out I was paralysed from the neck down and the problem was to find somewhere suitable to live. Despite the fact that they already had two children to look after, my friends Frank and Brenda suggested I stay with them. They invited me to their house for a trial period to see if they could cope. They found they could and I have been part of the family ever since.'

As he adjusted to his new mode of life John who had always been active found that time hung heavy on his hands. Like others who suffered similar and unexpected paralysis, he began to use a mouth stick for turning the pages of newspapers and books and this led to him attempting to write with a mouth-held pencil. As his confidence grew he looked about for more challenging activity and decided to try sewing using Brenda's sewing machine. His first objective was to make dresses for his two daughters. First he designed them and Brenda followed his drawings as she cut out the material which he then sewed on the machine, guiding the material with his mouth.

While he was working on the dresses a Welfare officer visited him and seeing what he was doing said that she could get him work sewing pillow cases for which he would be paid £1.50 per hundred. In the 'sixties disability payments were not as generous as they are today and John was always on a financial tightrope yet he felt the effort required to sew a pillow case using his mouth was worth more than just over three-and-a-half old pence and he declined the offer. But he still needed something more than 'dress-making' to occupy him so he tried repairing clocks!

This was not a success. Brenda was always afraid that he would swallow a spring or cogwheel but at least the attempt showed that John was gaining confidence in using his mouth in place of his hands.

'A visiting nurse used to tease me that I was idle and suggested that I took up art,' John says. 'She loaned me a couple of books on painting and brought along an artist friend who helped to set me up with what I needed. I found it very difficult at first and stuck to using a pencil. My first "work of art" was a donkey. A friend was arranging a children's party and one of the games she planned was pin-the-tail-on-the-donkey!

'One thing seemed to lead to another and next I was asked to paint a backcloth for a Sunday school nativity play. Brenda hung up a double bed sheet with weights at the bottom to keep it taut while I painted on it. I really enjoyed it and it was used year after year at the school.'

Following this he painted his first 'proper' picture, the wind-driven galleon which he gave as a present to his nurse.

Before his accident John had never dreamed of becoming an artist but now he spent many hours painting for his own pleasure.

What was frustrating at this time was the difficulty he had with his brushes. Holding the handles in his teeth he found he was inclined to chew through them.

One day Brenda returned home in triumph with some small bamboos which she had bought in a garden shop. With a brush fitted in one end, the light bamboo sticks proved ideal. But just when it seemed that John was at last well-equipped for his hobby he started to feel ill.

He explained to his nurse that he felt sick and terribly weak. While he was speaking she picked up one of his bamboo painting sticks.

"What do you know about these bamboo canes?" she asked. "Did you not realise that they are treated with chemicals for the garden? You have been poisoning yourself with them."

Regretfully John gave up his bamboos and immediately his health improved.

Great ingenuity was used in trying to find the perfect holder and everything was tried from the rubber stem of an electric kettle to plastic tubes but none was satisfactory.

Then he tried fitting the brush in pipe stems. This worked well until they were no longer available.

After that he noticed the mouthpiece that a disabled friend used with his POSM equipment and since then these special mouth pieces have provided him with the perfect brush holders.

In 1972 a nurse, who was raising money for charity, asked if she could take some of his pictures to a wine-and-cheese party she was holding. They were so well received that it was decided to hold an exhibition for the cause – twenty-five of John's pictures were shown of which twenty were sold.

A local newspaper carried a report on the work of the disabled painter and an unknown person sent the cutting to the Association of Mouth and Foot Painting Artists in London. John knew nothing of this until he received a letter from the Association expressing interest in his work. He immediately sent off six of his best paintings and soon he was invited to become a student.

'The grant from the Association transformed John's life,' Brenda told the author. 'It meant that he could afford a special battery-driven wheelchair which he was able to control himself so that at last he had freedom of movement. This was followed by a Renault Trafic van with special ramps so that he could take his wheelchair on board to be clamped securely in place in order to travel in comfort. He has used it to travel about to give lectures on this work and demonstrations to Women's Institutes. None of this could have been done on his sickness benefit.'

Another advantage of being a student was that John was able to have his own studio built on to the house where he lives at Norton Down Green some miles outside Bath. In this light and airy room he works for hours on end at his paintings, usually starting at 10.30 a.m. and working right through until 6 p.m. or later with only a break for a cup of tea.

John paints in oils and – like the artist Edward Burra – in water-colour applied so thickly that it almost has the effect of oil paint. His favourite subjects are animals and boats.

'I do not always find painting easy,' he admits. 'Sometimes I just look at the canvas for some hours and then suddenly I get an idea and away I go and I don't want to stop. This can present a problem because I cannot feel heat or cold – and I get too involved to check the temperature. The first thing I know is that my teeth are chattering with cold and I have to go to bed with hot water bottles.'

John looked upon 1992 as his 'Great Year'. It was then that he was made a full member of the Association.

'It was the best day in my life for twenty-seven years,' he says. 'I was able to return my DHSS book which gave me a great deal of satisfaction. At sixty-three years old I had realised that a hobby had turned into a full-time occupation which enabled me to enjoy a completely independent way of life. It also means that I am now able to help my three children and take out my young grandchildren. All this makes me realise that life doesn't end with a broken neck.'

Mojgan Safa

'I love my life.'

It was an Aladdin's Cave, a gallery of treasures but not of precious stones and ingots of gold. The treasures here hung on the walls, paintings that seemed to the awe-struck girl beyond the doorway to glow as though they contained an inner light. Slowly she ventured inside, her wheelchair squeaking on the polished floor as she used her leg to haul herself forward. An art class was in progress and the noise made a number of people turn and gaze at the intruder but the man in charge smiled at her and invited her to stay.

When the class was over he spoke to the pretty girl in the wheelchair who introduced herself as Mojgan Safa and explained that her parents had just changed their home and now had an apartment in the building above the gallery. Her father worked in the Iranian Ministry of Roads and Highways and the family had been frequently on the move but now they were back in Teheran. She had been exploring the new location when she looked through the door and had been attracted by the paintings. Seeing the class in progress had given her a wonderful idea...

The gallery director listened sympathetically as she told him that while her disability meant that she could only control one leg, she was adept at using her foot and toes as able-bodied people were at using their hands.

Would he consider teaching her to paint?

The man smiled at the eager fourteen-year-old and agreed. It would give this unfortunate something to do to pass her lonely hours he thought, not realizing that painting was to become the most important factor in her life.

In 1968 Mojgan's mother was seven months pregnant when the car in which she was riding was involved in an accident and overturned. Although she herself was unhurt she was fearful for the child she carried and immediately had a medical examination. Doctors reassured her that no harm had been done. But the confidence that their words inspired did not last when Mojgan was born a month prematurely and the midwife saw that the infant appeared to be black all over.

In Iran it was customary for babies to be born at home and the midwife did not have the oxygen equipment that should have been used immediately. Yet Mojgan survived and began to look more healthy, and at the time no one guessed that parts of her brain had been destroyed through lack of oxygen.

Seven months later Mojgan's mother again became anxious over the baby's condition. She did not follow moving objects with her eyes and it seemed impossible for her to hold her head erect. She was seen by local doctors and when they admitted there was nothing they could do Mojgan's parents took her to specialists in England and America. Their verdict was unanimous – it was impossible to cure the brain damage she had suffered at birth.

In Iran Mojgan grew up with her mother and father and though she had no control over her body it was obvious to her family that there was nothing wrong with her mentally, on the contrary she appeared to be unusually intelligent and capable of learning very quickly. She also developed remarkable control of the limb that had remained unaffected. Using her toes she sewed with needles and even used scissors to cut out material. Thus she had little difficulty in learning the technique of foot painting and visitors to her home watched in amazement when she used her toes to take the caps off tubes of oil paint, gently squeeze the required amount out on to a palette and mix it to the shade she wanted.

Towards the end of the 'eighties her family moved to London and took up residence in a West London flat. In 1988 an approach was made to the Association of Mouth and Foot Painting Artists and she was accepted as a student in May of the following year. It was soon after this that the author met her and as Mojgan had not learned English her cousin Vida acted as interpreter.

'She is very anxious to learn the language and I am sure she will take to it quickly,' Vida said. 'She is getting a computer with English-Arabic programmes and we think this will be of great help.

'Joining the AMFPA has given her a reason for living – the chance of a professional career. Her goal is to become a full member for apart from the satisfaction of artistic recognition it would make her mind easy over the future. At the moment her mother and father, who is now retired, devote themselves to looking after her but there is anxiety as to what will happen when they can no longer cope. Membership of the Association would mean that for the rest of her life she would be able to afford the necessary help to be independent.'

Hassan Movahhednia is an Iranian artist resident in Britain and each week he visited the Safa household to help Mojgan with her painting. For this she used a tilted table that Hassan made for her which stood on the floor at the right angle for her foot while she sat in her wheelchair.

'Technically she is perfect,' said Hassan. 'She can do everything including cleaning her own brushes. My role is to teach her composition and the significance of colours. When we come each week we talk about the work she has done, and my main aim is to convince her of her own ability, to give her the confidence to paint in her own way. There is something – a great feeling -inside her which she is somehow frightened to express. When I see a painting by Elizabeth Twistington Higgins I see in it Elizabeth herself, it could not be the work of anyone else. The whole thing about Elizabeth is in her canvases, and that is what I want for Mojgan – to put her individuality into her canvases.'

When the author met Mojgan again three years later there was no need for cousin Vida to interpret, Mojgan was fluent in English and in her animated style had no difficulty in bringing him up to date on the happenings in her life.

'When I joined the Association I felt like I had been born again because there was something to work towards in the future,' she said. 'I wanted to be independent so the first thing was to learn the English language. I went to a lesson and this was my first time in any class or school and I enjoyed myself so much. I attended the Keith Grove Project, a school for the disabled, five mornings and one afternoon a week and I also attended an adult education college three afternoons a week. In the evenings I painted.

'I wanted to change my life and now I am going to take a two-year Foundation course in an art college after which I want to work for a degree in art. I know it will not be easy but I do not think it will be too difficult either. I have found that I can cope and I have started to enjoy myself. I have been on holiday with ADKC – that's Action for Disability Kensington and Chelsea. At first my parents were worried – and so was I because it was my first time away from home but I had to go because I wanted to. I surprised myself and keep on surprising myself.

'I am disabled but it is nothing – I want to try everything.'

When the author left after seeing the remarkable progress Mojgan had made with her painting, her last words to him were, 'I love my life.'

Grant Sharman

'How fortunate I am'

'It was the beginning of a rather traumatic change in my life,' says Grant Sharman when describing the accident he suffered at the age of fifteen. The only son of parents who had emigrated from England to New Zealand in the late 'fifties, he was enrolled in King's College Boys School, Auckland, in 1975. Here he found the only sport he really enjoyed playing was Rugby and though he gave his all to the game he is emphatic that he was not a reckless player.

On 6 July 1977 he was playing as a tighthead prop in an inter-house game when he was thrown out of the ruck.

'I got so carried away on this one occasion that I dived back into the ruck without thinking, my head got wedged between two players and then the ruck collapsed,' he says. 'It was as though the world had collapsed.'

Like Trevor Wells who suffered a similar accident in England, Grant had broken his neck playing the sport he loved – and like Trevor, still does.

He was taken to the Middlemore Hospital which was only a mile away and here skull tongs were fitted to his head – 'Horrible things!' After nine weeks his neck was operated on, wire being put round the vertebra and bone grated on to either side. Five weeks later he became the first patient to be admitted to the Otara Spinal Unit, Otahuhu, which was to be his home for the next decade.

'I was very shaky when I was put in a wheelchair and I was still weak when I resumed my education,' he recalls. 'I could only manage two University Entrance subjects English and Physics which I studied as a pupil of the New Zealand Correspondence School the next year.'

This remarkable institution – of which the author was once a grateful pupil – was established to educate disabled children or those who lived on farms too remote to attend school, by mail and radio programmes.

When he came to take his exams he sat in front of a typewriter tapping the keys with a stick taped to his wrists and after six hours of this he was so exhausted that he swore he would never go through such an ordeal again. But the effort was worth it. He passed and the following year he took chemistry and maths. In 1980 he did courses in English and the History of Art and finally completed a paper on economics through Massey University. But while he enjoyed studying he had to face the fact he did not know what he wanted to do with his life.

Five years after his accident Grant had recovered enough strength to drive a car specially equipped for a quadriplegic. A surgeon told him that now he was mobile he should get a job. Grant took his advice and became a receptionist for two days a week at Vision Wallpapers, Paptoetoe, where he was able to drive himself to work from the unit.

'I was very nervous at first in my wheelchair,' he remembers, 'but that job was a great turning point in my life. It was tremendous to be with people in an ordinary situation and it gave me confidence. to do a lot of things. Until then I felt useless but now I had a job to do and I did it. I was particularly touched when the staff arranged a 21st birthday party for me at the office.'

Meanwhile Grant had met a member of the Mouth and Foot Painting Artists' Association named Bruce Hopkins who asked him if he would like to try painting with a mouth-held brush.

'Bruce, I can't hold a brush in my mouth,' Grant protested.

'That's not a problem,' replied Bruce who was renowned for his confident nature. 'Just stick it in your mouth and away you go.'

Grant laughed and under Bruce's instruction attempted to paint – and was completely discouraged.

'It was a pathetic effort,' he admits. 'I just wanted to throw it away but Bruce was very persuasive and the next night I was attempting to paint again. This time there was the slightest improvement but more importantly I was enjoying it and decided to keep trying, greatly encouraged by Bruce and my mother and father

'Later on, Bruce suggested that I should submit six of my paintings to the Association of Mouth and Foot Painting Artists. This I did only to have them returned with a note saying that the paintings were not suitable for their requirements.'

Grant was so disappointed he felt he had 'been kicked in the teeth', but the rejection had the effect of making him more determined than before. He changed his style of painting and when he was satisfied that he had improved he sent off another half dozen pictures and waited nervously for the verdict.

When the reply arrived in January 1981 and was opened for him it contained wonderful news. Grant says, 'I was really proud to sign a contract as a student of the Association. It was only after I had done this I saw the potential of art to give me my elusive independence. I had something to focus on, and I remember my father saying, "if you become a full member you will have an income guaranteed for life." And I thought, "There are not many people, able-bodied or disabled, that that can happen to." And so I worked and worked.'

Although he did try hard he did not make the progress he had hoped. As a student he was able to have tuition but the two teachers he had for periods during the next five years did not take him in the direction he felt he should go. As a result he remained mainly self-taught and he felt disappointed in the lack of success that he wanted so desparately.

Early in 1986 this changed when a professional artist named Doreen Jones, a pleasant South African lady with a halo of snow white hair, came to the spinal unit and watched Grant at work in front of his easel.

'She just watched me but made no comment,' he says. 'Then she came again and went away, but on her third visit she said, "Can I help?" Thanks to her everything began to happen. It was like being a diamond encrusted in rock and she broke away the chips. My paintings changed almost immediately, becoming more detailed and professional as she taught me nearly everything I know!

'I owe Doreen a lot of credit because she showed me how to tackle subjects I thought were nearly impossible – bush scenes, ships in full detail and other complicated subjects which was great because I wanted to be a painter who could paint realistically – *I wanted people to see what I had painted come off the canvas!*

'My breakthrough came when I painted an eagle. When I had finished it appeared as though it was about to fly out of the picture. As I looked at it I felt that at last I was getting somewhere in the art world. This feeling was endorsed in late 1987 when I received a letter to say that I had been accepted as a full member of the Association of Mouth and Foot Painting Artists. I shall never forget sitting in my room by myself and re-reading that letter and realizing that I had finally achieved something.'

Bruce Hopkins, who so cheerfully introduced Grant to painting, had died in 1985 which meant that Grant was the only full member of the Association in New Zealand though there were several students some of whom were in the spinal unit. This situation gave him a sense of responsibility. In the Association's regular journal circulated to members and students around the world there was very little mention of New Zealand artists and it became Grant's priority to put his country on the map as far as disabled artists were concerned.

'We had done very little,' he admits, 'but I like to think that in the last few years we have achieved a lot. Our work has been published overseas in America and Canada, Holland, Australia and France and I feel that we are now contributing to the global AMFPA.'

One of the things that caused Grant much thought when he became a professional painter was that he felt he was not a 'natural' artist and he wondered what it was that had enabled him to achieve the degree of proficiency required to become a member.

'When I had my accident my housemaster rode in the ambulance with me to hospital,' Grant says. 'After that he kept in touch and became like an elder brother. At the time religion meant little to me but because he became converted I began to take an interest in it. In 1980 I became a Christian and I do believe that had a great deal to do with my success.

'I was very impressed with a book I read by Joni Eareckson, an amazing artist paralysed from the neck down after a diving accident who now travels the world lecturing and singing. When she signs a painting she puts the letters PTL beneath her signature – PTL standing for "Praise the Lord". And I figure that He has a big hand in the way I paint and now I put the same initials on my work.'

Apart from his painting, Grant still enjoys Rugby, watching games at Eden Park when he can. One of his most pleasurable moments was visiting the dressing-room of the home team when Auckland won the Ranfurly Shield from Canterbury – and it takes a New Zealander to appreciate the almost mystic significance of the shield.

Grant had been in the spinal unit for ten years when he became a member and as a result he was able to have a two-bedroomed cottage built to his own specification at the back of his parents' house in Papakura. The doors were made wide enough for his wheelchair and the kitchen and bathroom were designed specially for his use. Best of all was his studio with large windows so that for the first time he was able to work in what he termed 'splendid light'. Here he enjoyed the daily company of his parents, his father often coming into the studio – according to Grant – to tell him that his painting wasn't coming right. And here his friend Jenny Anderson, a nurse he met in the Spinal Unit, put out his paints for him and helped with preparations for demonstrations and exhibitions.

There was another companion who spent a great deal of time with Grant in the studio and that was his cat Tom who has appeared on a calendar. It was a sad time for Grant when faithful Tom departed this world. Today his feline friends are the kittens Napoleon (Poly) and Josephine (Jo) who follow Tom's tradition of companionship when Grant is painting, and also have the habit of putting their paws in paints.

Grant moved into his new home in February 1988, revelling in the pleasure of his new-found independence. But it was not long before the Otara Spinal Unit contacted him and asked if he would go back two days a week to counsel new patients.

'If you have broken your neck or your back and you have a lot of questions to ask,' explains Grant. 'An able-bodied person is not so plausible as someone in a wheelchair – when the session is over they don't get up and walk away, they wheel away.'

Like some other disabled artists in this book Grant makes a point of giving talks and demonstrations in schools and to interested organisations. In order to gain confidence he joined the Toastmasters, an international society which promotes public speaking and debating. It is an activity that he finds thoroughly enjoyable, competing successfully in debating teams and winning a couple of competitions.

'Being nervous in public is something I have overcome,' he says. 'I still had my mind and the ability to speak. I remember when I was a student giving a demonstration of mouth painting with Bruce Hopkins in Auckland and I was absolutely terrified. Last year I painted in an arcade in Queen Street – Auckland's best known thoroughfare. One moment there was no one watching me, the next there were fifty onlookers and I wasn't scared at all. I just wanted to show people how we paint, that we are not vegetables but ordinary people who can't walk.

'It is acceptance that one strives for – to be seen not as a disabled artist but as an artist fullstop. That came to fruition for me in 1989 when I entered for the Waitakere Licensing Trust Award in which I won a merit award for a painting of a tiger.'

In 1993 Grant won the Bruce Hopkins Memorial Art Award with a painting of two young boys sitting on Rugby balls watching a game of Rugby.

'The award was established after Bruce's death and I was thrilled to win it especially as Bruce introduced me to mouth painting and the MFPA,' says Grant who now lives in a small rural community called Wai Pa with his friend Jenny who is now Mrs Sharman. Together they had a house built with a spacious studio on a ten-acre site.

'It is a marvellous place in which to paint and live and we are very happy,' Grant declares. 'I think I am an incredibly lucky person. Of course there are times when I get a bit low, when things don't go right, but then I think about how fortunate I am and I snap out of it. To me the great thing about being an artist is that we do spread some enjoyment and give to others instead of always receiving, and we do get to leave a bit of ourselves behind when we go.'

Tom Yendell

'Great Fun!'

When Tom Yendell begins a painting he has to decide whether to hold the brush in his teeth or his toes. One of those affected by the drug thalidomide he has the rare ability to be both a foot and a mouth painting artist. He has many other talents that he uses in the service of others and this was recognized when he was chosen as one of the twelve Men of the Year in 1986.

Tom was born without arms in 1962 when his parents lived in Basingstoke. Before long the family moved to Leighton Buzzard where Tom's father had a bakery. A few years later Mr. Yendell became ill with arthritis and when the Lady Hoare Trust, which was concerned with thalidomide sufferers, required someone to run its holiday home in Pevensey, East Sussex, he and his wife took the job. Here Tom went to a local primary school but as he did not appear to be doing well there he was enrolled at a prep school at the age of nine.

A year-and-a-half later he went to Treloar College at Alton in Hampshire. This establishment catering for the disabled was to have a significant influence upon his life. When Tom joined it had eighty students; today it is the biggest school for the handicapped in Britain with just under three hundred young people who are nearly all boarders. At Treloar they study an 'able-bodied' syllabus and sit for GCSEs and A-Levels.

Tom studied the 'normal subjects' for seven years at Treloar and at the end of that time decided that the only subject he was any good at was art. ('Academically I was not that bright at school,' he admits cheerfully.) He therefore went to the Hastings College of Art to do a year's foundation course in art after which he applied to Canterbury to do fine art and Brighton to do expressive art. He was accepted by both colleges and he chose Brighton Polytechnic to be near his parents who were now living in Bexhill.

At the same time he had the satisfaction of passing his driving test and owning his first car, a Mini which was specially modified.

After two years of studying for his degree Tom was finding it hard to concentrate and felt the need to change his occupation for a while. Taking sabbatical year he worked for the charity CRYPT – Creative Young People Together – which helped disabled youngsters with artistic talents and provided them with accommodation in bungalows around the country. Such work with fellow handicapped persons has been a theme of Tom's life ever since.

For the second half of his sabbatical year Tom went back to Treloar College. Here he worked in the art room with his old teacher who unfortunately died leaving Tom to carry on the classes until the end of the term.

Tom returned to Brighton where much of his work involved photography. He had to use a tripod to hold his camera and he found it very difficult to focus the lens. The only way he could do it was by bending down and using his feet while he looked through the viewfinder. He came up with an idea for a shoulder attachment which he designed and manufactured with John Downie an engineer from the Polytechnic. The equipment gives him mobility with his camera which he easily operates with his chin and mouth.

When he had obtained his degree Tom looked around for work and found a job with Business in the Community, an organization connected with enterprise agencies and new small businesses. He enjoyed the work but after eight months found that travelling up to London each day from his home in Lewes was a strain and he looked about for something else.

When he had been doing his foundation course in art he had contacted the Association of Mouth and Foot Painting Artists and had been told to get in touch again after he had got his degree. Now he did so and in March 1986 became a student of the Association.

Soon after this he bought an old house on the Sussex Downs with the delightful name of 'Hunter's Moon' which was in need of renovation.

'It had a great studio at the bottom of the garden' says Tom. 'And I really enjoyed doing it up. You see I was planning to get married to Lucy, who I had met the year before when she was doing her foundation course in art. The house was to be ready for Lucy when she finished her art degree in graphics and illustration at Bath.'

While he was having the house renovated, and painting for the Association, Tom still found time to do voluntary work for maladjusted children at the local school. It was for helping others that he was chosen as one of the Men of the Year that November which entailed travelling to London to receive his citation in company with such well known figures as Frank Bruno, Bob Monkhouse and Richard Branson.

On the eighth day of the eighth month 1988 Tom and Lucy were married – Tom saying he had chosen the date of 8.8.88 as he would easily remember his wedding anniversary. The couple went to Iceland for their honeymoon.

'Lucy is mad about Iceland,' says Tom, 'but I was rather apprehensive about going. It turned out to be a wonderful experience and now I would like to go again. We spent seven days touring the country and the rest of the time in Reykjavik. I was so impressed by the Icelandic attitude to the disabled. There they have a national Union of Disabled People which owns a specially designed building – complete with a "bank" of carers, a gym, swimming pool and craft room – where the disabled can rent apartments. Everything is run by the disabled even to having their own taxi service.'

In 1989 Tom returned to Treloar College to take up the newly created position of part-time activities co-ordinator which he thoroughly enjoyed even though it meant that he and Lucy had to leave 'Hunter's Moon' in order to live in Alton. Their new house is named 'Thule' which was the ancient name for Iceland.

Being part-time the work allowed Tom time to do his own painting which these days he does mostly with a mouth-held brush. When he was small he used his feet as his 'hands' but when he went as a young student to Treloar College he found that this method of working was inconvenient as the tables there were not suitable to sit on and so he changed to holding his brush or pen in his mouth.

'Although I mostly paint by mouth I can still use my foot,' he explains, 'especially when I use charcoal which does not taste very nice. I use water-colours for my painting but what I enjoy most is working black and white. You can get such marvellous effects with black ink. I give talks and demonstrations at schools and at the Association's last exhibition in London I had school kids sitting on the floor writing with their feet. Great fun!'

Another of Tom's ideas of fun is to go skiing in Switzerland which is the result of Lucy's encouragement. He has had a holiday in Gstaad where he skied with the British Ski Team.

'I love it,' he declares, 'I even love falling down!'

Today Tom is the busy curator of the MFPA Gallery in the famous Hampshire village of Selborne. It was set up by the Association to provide a permanent area to exhibit the work of disabled artists and where members of the public can see one of the MFPA artists at work.

Trevor Wells

'I was amazed – I was painting!'

Breezy used to be one of the most over-worked adjectives that journalists coined to describe certain buoyant characters yet this cliche word could not be bettered when applied to Trevor Wells. His characteristic expression is a happy smile and when the tape of the author's interview with him is replayed it is punctuated by gusts of laughter.

Some might think that Trevor has little to laugh about being paralysed and without feeling from the mid-chest down since he suffered an accident when he was twenty-one. Yet his view of life is remarkably positive, especially since he discovered an unsuspected talent for painting.

'As far as I was concerned at school the art period was a lesson in which you did as little as possible,' he says. 'All I was really interested in was sport. I was mad about it – still am, strangely enough, though now I can only watch. When I left school I became a carpenter with a building firm and I used to play with a Rugby club in Uxbridge.'

In September 1978 he set out with his team to play a Sunday match – a 'beer match' as such games are known within the fraternity – at the grounds of the Twickenham Rugby Club.

'I did not take it as seriously as I should have done,' he explains. 'It was a hot Indian summer and we were not keyed up before the game as usually happens. Indeed we put our boots on out on the pitch which you never do normally.

'There was a drop out and then a scrum and in it I was too late in getting my head down. I was trapped and took the weight of the scrum on the back of my neck.'

When the scrum broke up Trevor was unable to move. An ambulance was called and he was taken to the Middlesex Hospital, and the same evening moved to London's Charing Cross Hospital for spinal fusion. He had broken his neck at the C4 level.

From Charing Cross Hospital Trevor was taken to Stoke Mandeville Hospital where he spent the next six months, a period of great adjustment for a young man who had lived for sport and who within seconds had been condemned to a life of immobility.

'I must confess I did a lot of heavy thinking there,' he says, 'but I like to think that I did not find it too difficult to come to terms with my disability. Of course it's hard to say so yourself but I realized that I must not have the attitude of some who felt that the whole world was against them because of an accident. I knew I had to carry on but, as I said, there were times for some pretty deep thought.'

In April 1979 Trevor was transferred to the recently opened Alderbourne Unit at Hillingdon Hospital in Uxbridge which was designed for such long-term cases and there he lived in a pleasant informal atmosphere. He had his own room and thanks to an electric wheelchair was able to move about.

'I went there because I knew that having to cope with a quadriplegic was too much of a burden on my mother,' he explains.

Having accepted the fact that everything had altered so drastically Trevor was able to adapt to life in the Alderbourne Unit. His interest in sport was undiminished and he certainly felt no bitterness against the game which was the cause of his accident. He watched every minute of sport that appeared on television and read newspapers, especially the sporting sections. In order to turn the pages he learned to used a mouthstick.

'And so the days flowed by just doing nothing,' he says. 'Then ten years ago someone suggested that I should have a go at painting. It was something that I had never ever considered, the last thing at which I thought I would be any good. But I decided to try to pass the time and I was set up with paints and a brush fitted to my mouth-stick. I must say the results at first were iffy to say the least but I became interested enough to keep going. By the time I was on my third picture I was quite amazed. I was actually painting!'

Trevor found little difficulty in manipulating his mouthstick, especially after getting one specially adapted. Remembering his Rugby days when he used a gum shield, he had an extra-light arrow shaft fitted to such a shield. The beauty of the device is that it holds the stick with a brush or pen attached perfectly steady while distributing the weight in Trevor's mouth. In this way no strain is placed on his teeth and he does not have the fatigue of having to clench them. It is so successful that his mouth writing is better than his old handwriting.

When discussing his painting Trevor makes it sound as if it is one of the easiest things in the world.

'It is so simple – there are so few rules,' he says. 'You just have to remember that you start with the background and work forward, that light against dark throws colour up and so on.'

Such basics he worked out for himself. He never had a tutor though when he had been painting for a couple of years he tried an Adult Education course for beginners in art. This did little to help him as through hard work and experiment he was far from being a beginner.

Although the idea of becoming a professional painter did not then occur to Trevor his fascination with painting drove him on to improve his technique. He began using oil paint which he liked because 'you can move it round a bit even after a couple of days' but like other mouth-painting artists he found there were drawbacks. Brushes were difficult for him to clean and the smell of oil and turpentine gave him bad headaches. He changed over to water-colours and then found what he was looking for with acrylic paints. Although they have many of the properties of oil paints they can be mixed with water. Their main difference with oils is the dramatically shorter drying time which means the artist has to get it right within a matter of minutes.

Trevor found a direction for his art when relatives of a fellow patient at Alderbourne saw his work. By coincidence they knew the foot-painting artist Paul Driver and suggested to Trevor that he should send samples of his work to the organization to which Paul belonged. Although he had never heard of the Association of Mouth and Foot Painting Artists he followed this advice, with the result that he was offered a studentship and within two-and-a-half years was accepted as a member.

'Through its marketing the Association makes it possible for me to earn my living with my paint brush,' Trevor says. 'I certainly could not survive on my own but by being a member of the partnership I have the benefit of its commercial outlets.' In return Trevor concentrates on subjects which he knows are suitable for the Association to market.

'I am lucky in that what I like painting and what is commercial are combined,' he says. 'It takes me a long time to complete a picture and I can see no point in working up to four months on a painting if it is not suitable for printing.'

Four months may seem a long time even for a mouth-painter until you see Trevor's work. His outdoor scenes are made up of the most amazing detail which gives the impression that every leaf on every tree is painstakingly painted as an individual part of the whole. To achieve this his brushes are so fine that he laughingly claims that some only have a couple of hairs. The result is that his paintings have a startling clarity.

'Although I go for "printable" subjects I never paint a picture that I could not hang up on my wall,' he declares. 'I like to do scenes that you could walk into.'

And here is the clue to Trevor's success. Though he is immobile physically his inner eye roams free in the landscape he is creating. The author, who lives close to Hadrian's Wall in the north of England and is used to the sight of snowy fells, could almost feel the cold emanate from one of Trevor's paintings depicting a winter scene in Cumbria.

He is particularly known for his mastery of snow in his pictures.

'I do like snow,' he agrees, 'and with the light which reflects you can get some lovely effects. Winter transforms everything and to me there is something magical about snowdrifts with the footmarks of animals printed on them, even tyre marks on a snow-covered road.'

And there is another reason why Trevor likes to do such paintings. They do not require much red paint and he has mild colour blindness when it comes to reds and greens, not that anyone could guess it when seeing an exhibition of his work.

In July 1990 Trevor was able to leave the Alderbourne Unit and the next year set up home with his new wife Shirley who was his osteopath. Through becoming a professional artist he has attained an independence which he could not imagine when he lay in Stoke Mandeville Hospital and pondered on what life could hold for someone who would never be able to leave his wheelchair.

'It is curious,' he muses. 'No way would I have become an artist if that accident had not happened.'

HEATHER STRUDWICK *Pas De Deux*

HEATHER STRUDWICK
The One That Got Away
Oil

HEATHER STRUDWICK   *Mistlee Creek*   Oil   30 x 41 cm

122

EDWARD RAINEY   *Church in Snow*   Oil   61 x 45 cm

JOHN SAVAGE
Winter Snows
Oil   36 x 25 cm

JOHN SAVAGE   *'City of Birmingham'*   Oil   36 x 46 cm

JOHN SAVAGE   'Swan Lake'   Oil   30 x 41 cm

JOHN SAVAGE   Village in the Snow   Oil   31 x 46 cm

MOJGAN SAFA   *Abstract*   Oil   30 x 20 cm

MOJGAN SAFA   *Window*   Oil   30 x 46 cm

GRANT SHARMAN
Climbing Roses
Watercolour   40 x 27 cm

GRANT SHARMAN
Wild Flowers
Watercolour   42 x 30 cm

GRANT SHARMAN   *Winter Stagecoach*   Oil   45 x 60 cm

GRANT SHARMAN   *Waterfall Reserve*   Oil   46 x 60 cm

TOM YENDELL   *Roses*   Watercolour   50 x 38 cm

TOM YENDELL
Flowers
Coloured Pencils   50 x 40 cm

TOM YENDELL
Carol Singers
Watercolour   31 x 30 cm

TREVOR WELLS *The Falls of Dochart, Central Scotland* Acrylic 46 x 56 cm

TREVOR WELLS *Loch Laggan at Sunset, Scottish Highlands*
Acrylic 46 x 61 cm

TREVOR WELLS *The Seven Sisters, East Sussex* Acrylic 45 x 61 cm

TREVOR WELLS   *The Boat House*   Oil   36 x 46 cm

TREVOR WELLS   *Winter Walk*   Acrylic   41 x 51 cm

Overleaf: TREVOR WELLS   *Cley Mill, Norfolk*   Acrylic   40 x 51 cm

133

TREVOR WELLS   *Grassmere, Lake District*   Oil 46 x 61 cm

TREVOR WELLS   *Winter Cottage*   Oil 46 x 56 cm

136

Myron Angus

'For moral courage'

Everyone watched with curiosity tinged with awe as the armless man bent his head forward and signed his name with a mouth-held pen on the fly leaf of the book entitled *My Desire* which he had written in the same laborious way. The year was 1933, the venue a huge exhibition in Toronto, Ontario, and the author's name was Bill Watson. Although he did not know it at the time, he achieved much more than selling a pile of books that day.

In the crowd that pressed round him was a couple who had a passionate interest in what they saw, and when the first rush of book purchasers had departed with their uniquely signed copies they approached the author. They introduced themselves as Mr and Mrs Angus from St Mary's, and explained that when their son Myron had been born seven years earlier his hands, arms and legs were completely paralysed. All he could do was sit at home, frustrated at not being able to play like the other children he saw from his window or go to school. Could Mr Watson, from his own experience of disability, proffer any advice...

Bill Watson certainly could.

First of all he autographed a copy of his book specially for Myron and then he said, 'Put a pencil between his teeth. Let him hold it on either the left or right side, whichever way is the most comfortable, and let him learn to write with it. And once he has mastered that, put him in school – they can't refuse to teach him.'

On their journey back to St Mary's the couple eagerly discussed what they had seen and been told. At last it seemed there was a glimmer of hope for Myron – if a man who had no arms had managed to write a book it might be possible for their son to receive a normal education.

At home Myron was given the book *My Desire* as proof of what might be accomplished and his father bought pencils and pads by the dozen for the boy to attempt to form letters. As with so many mouth painters, the first attempts at controlling a pencil or brush clamped between the teeth were often disappointing. For one thing the eyes have to be so close to the paper that it is difficult to get an overall picture of what one is doing and eye strain is a common complaint with those who are forced to write and draw by this method. And then there is the question of control, just when it seems that a word has been written satisfactorily an involuntary head movement will send the pencil point skidding off at a tangent.

But even at the age of seven Myron was aware of how necessary his 'feeble attempts', as he later called them, were if he was going to free himself from the limitations of disability. He never gave up trying and was rewarded by the ability to write as clearly as his non-handicapped peers.

'It was as if a whole new door had suddenly opened in front of me,' Myron says today. 'And I was lucky to go to a regular school. I think it is a big thing not to get labelled as "different."'

His success as a student at a school where everyone else was able-bodied was recognized in 1940 when he was awarded a medal at his High School in St. Mary's, a medal inscribed with the words 'For Moral Courage'.

A year later the Angus family moved to Toronto where Myron was to complete his formal education at Riverdale Collegiate. In those days the needs of the disabled were not as widely recognized as today and the college did not have the facilities for students such as Myron. However, the staff went out to their way to accommodate him and he was actually carried from room to room.

During this period Myron had become increasingly interested in the idea of drawing and painting. He dearly wanted to attend an art school so that his attempts with a mouth-held brush could be given professional guidance but, as with his college, the art establishments were not geared to the requirement of someone so disabled and were certainly not as sympathetic as the Riverdale Collegiate.

'I was fascinated with colour, line and form,' he recalls. 'And as I was unable to receive formal art training I set about teaching myself, at first by copying illustrations from the family Bible and the works of Old Masters. I was determined to settle for no less than my best and my work became my passion.'

When he finished college Myron was single-minded in his efforts to find employment in order to support himself, not necessarily the easiest objective for someone wheelchair-bound let alone wheelchair-bound without the use of their arms. Yet he managed, and in this it was his enthusiasm for painting that clinched the job. He started work in a garage looking after the books with a mouth-held pen – and painting lettering and logos on the door panels of trucks.

Many a truck owner was astonished to walk into the busy garage to see a young man in a wheelchair and with a long-handled brush in his mouth decorating the side of his vehicle. It might not be art as taught in colleges but it certainly gave Myron as sense of self confidence.

But while he added up figures and did sign-painting during his working hours he continued to practice at what he believed was his true vocation – to become an artist.

In 1948 he felt he had progressed enough to mount his first exhibition.

It was held in a gallery on Yonge Street, Toronto, and was an instant success. So many people wanted to see the work of the young mouth painter that they had to queue in the street. Stories appeared the the Press not only about the technique he used but praising his delicate landscapes that reflected his love of the lakes and woods around Toronto. Other exhibitions followed in major cities in Canada and the USA.

Eleven years after his first exhibition Myron bought the gallery on Yonge Street where he not only exhibited and sold his own works but those of artists who had suffered disability like himself. The gallery proved to be a success – and it needed to be because Myron had married and he and his wife Alma had a young family to care for.

In 1963 news of Myron and his work crossed the Atlantic and came to the attention of the Association of Mouth and Foot Painting Artists at its headquarters in Liechtenstein. Samples of his work were requested and the independent committee of art experts who appraise the work of potential members was duly impressed. The next year Myron was elected a full member of the Association.

One result of this was that he found himself helping to organise an AMFPA exhibition at Toronto's Casa Loma during October 1965. At this exhibition over 150 paintings by the Association's members were put on display. It gave Myron the opportunity to meet the organisation's founder Erich Stegmann who, as a living example of how the disabled can rise above their physical adversities, received an ovation from the guests at the preview.

Four years later Myron found himself flying to India as the representative of Canadian and United States mouth and foot painting artists for a Delegates' Convention being held in Bombay. The artist had come a long way since the days he painted signs on trucks.

Thanks to the financial independence gained as a result of AMFPA membership Myron was able to give up the running of his gallery and devote his whole attention to art and a venture that had long occupied his thoughts. Mindful of his own early struggles to overcome the handicap that fate had laid upon him, he wished to help all handicapped persons to live fuller lives. To do this he planned to travel about Canada giving lectures and demonstrations that would encourage the disabled and at the same time give the able-bodied a better understanding of those physically less fortunate than themselves.

Rehabilitation centres, children's hospitals, service clubs, church groups, schools and gaols all provided venues for Myron's message, the only problem was that travelling to them by train and plane was expensive and difficult, especially as at that time hotels were not accessible for wheelchairs. Then a friend suggested that a motorhome might be the answer – and it proved to be the ideal means of travel for his unique roadshow.

For over twenty years Myron – helped by his wife Alma, daughter Theresa and sons Earl and Kevin – has devoted his spare time to his crusade in the cause of the disabled.

In particular he has sought to encourage others, both young and old, who have recently become disabled to take their place in society so that they will become the able disabled.

Myron has also served on the Ontario Advisory Council for the Physically Disabled. As a result of all these activities he has received many awards including the Vanier Medal for his achievements in painting, penmanship, and humanitarian services, and the *Legion des Gens de Coeur* from Paris for human courage. To date he has been interviewed on over 360 television programmes while over eight hundred newspapers and magazines around the world have carried features on his life and work

At his home in Port Stanley, Ontario, Myron continues to paint with undiminished enthusiasm, though he now mainly uses water colours as they are lighter to use than oils which put a strain on his teeth while gripping the brush. He often works under the critical gaze of his beautiful Siamese cat who, while accepting the fact the Myron is unable to stroke him, raises his chin so that his neck can be tickled with the end of a mouth stick.

'Yet if it had not been for the inspiration I received from Bill Watson in the 'Thirties I may never have been educated,' he says reflectively. And, like another artist in this book, he sums up his basic philosophy in eight words, 'Although one door may close another may be opened.'

Iwao Adachi

'Memories are all but sad. But I have my wife to share the worthwhileness of life, my daughter, who gives me the energy for tomorrow, and the painting that supports myself.'

So wrote Iwao Adachi to the author. In those few words this remarkable Japanese artist sums up his life – a life that has been made up of light and shade. On the light side he has known great success as a painter, on the dark a time when he stood in front of an oncoming locomotive because life seemed too grim to continue.

He was born in 1939 in Osaka where he lived happily with his parents until their house was burnt down in an air raid. The family then moved to the home of his mother's sister from where the boy went to school which he thoroughly enjoyed, especially playing baseball. One day when he was in the third grade his teacher told the class, 'If you feed birds from chicks they will remain tame – sparrows or doves, all are the same.'

When Iwao was walking home from school with his friends when one suggested they should find some sparrow chicks which they could rear as pets. The band of boys was passing the electrical substation at Kintetsu Yato-no-sato, and the boys saw sparrow nests high on an iron pylon. To the other boys the nest seemed too high to reach but they dared Iwao to climb up – and though inwardly reluctant the dare was something that he could not refuse.

He climbed up and when close to a nest he called down, 'There are sparrow chicks here.' Then everything blacked out.

Afterwards his friends told him that he did not actually touch the 33,000 volt high tension cable but he was engulfed in a shower of blue sparks and plunged to earth head first. As he lay crumpled on the ground they believed that he was dead.

When Iwao came round swathed in bandages the first thing he was aware of were the faces of his mother and father staring anxiously down at him. Behind them crowded hospital doctors, policemen and news reporters and, something that remained in his mind, his aunt glaring at him with an angry expression.

'Doctors said that it was a miracle that I survived,' Iwao says today. 'The electric current ran through my body from my right hand creating a hole in my abdomen the size of my fist while my head was injured as a result of the fall. And all my body was burned black.'

Iwao's right hand was amputated and then in two more operations he lost his right arm from the shoulder and his left below the elbow. When he was discharged four months later his homecoming was not the joyous occasion one usually expects in such circumstances.

'It was miserable because it was as though I was a piece of wood,' he says. 'My mother burst into tears and my father looked away from me and kept silent. I was unable to go to school so it no longer meant anything to me. I could not dress myself or eat – I could not live without my mother's help even for a single day. Yet the body is a curious creation and for some time I had the illusion that I still had my hands, I even felt my fingers itch.'

A year later a second tragedy struck the eleven-year-old boy. His mother, on whom he had become so dependent, died of a heart attack. She had suffered from a heart condition and it is believed that her son's dreadful accident aggravated it.

'I had thought that she would always be beside me but she was no more,' says Iwao. 'I felt I should have done something good for her while she was alive, even without hands

I should have done something for her. Tears ran down my face and I could not wipe them away.

'Shortly afterwards my father left. I was not surprised because he used to change his job frequently and was sometimes away for long periods, but it meant that I was left alone in my aunt's house. She was a hard person and did not help me as my mother had.

'I remember one day how I struggled to put on my trousers by myself. I was lying on the floor, trying to work my way into them, when my friends dropped in to see me on their way to school.

'"What are you doing like that?" they demanded.

'I was surprised and felt ashamed, and I tried to stand up in a hurry and as I did so my trousers dropped to my ankles. What a bad mannered sight I was. My friends frowned at me and left, I restarted work with my trousers. After two hours I had worked them up to my hip but I could not managed the hook – my mouth could not reach it. If only my mother could have been there! Tears of vexation filled my eyes. My aunt was in the next room but she never tried to help me.

'I could picture the vivid scene in the classroom, hear the happy shouting in the playground while I was left alone to struggle with my trousers.

'Then, by pressing my belly to the corner of a desk and using what remained of my left arm, I managed to fix the hook. My joy at this achievement was but a passing moment. There came the need to go to the toilet and I found that to undo the hook was as hard as it had been to fix it. At the last moment I rushed into the water closet. There the thought of having to struggle to get my trousers up again made me cry. I just wanted to sit there forever...

'After a while a friend visited me on the way back from school and found me standing in my underpants.'"What's the matter with you?" he asked. "You are still as you were. What have you done the whole day?"

'I tried to put on my trousers...'

'I could find no more words.'

The humiliation that the boy felt at not being able to look after himself had the effect of making him strive to be independent. The result was that he taught himself to do most of the everyday things of life including needlework and drawing by using his mouth.

This was inspired by his father once telling him the story of Junkyo Ohishi which he never forgot. One of the most remarkable of the remarkable band of mouth painters, Junkyo Ohishi died in 1968 at the age of eighty having spent many years of her life as a third-rank Buddhist priestess in the temple district of Bukoin in Kyoto. Apart from her delicate paintings, she was to be seen everyday copying from the Cannon-sutra with a mouth-held brush. Junkyo lost her hands at the age of seventeen when in a fit of insanity her adopted father attacked those about him with a sword. Later she said, 'One day I saw a small bird feeding its youngster with its beak. That was what prompted me to learn to write and draw with my mouth.'

A member of the Association of Mouth and Foot painting artists Junkyo was famous for her Buddhist compassion and opened a home offering sheltered accommodation for handicapped children.

Following the example of Junkyo, Iwao turned to drawing whenever he felt lonely or found life hard.

'In the year that my mother passed away I began to draw pictures,' Iwao recalls. 'It was to release my sorrow and to practice the use of my mouth. At first I tried to draw straight lines, triangles or squares – it took me a year to be able to draw straight lines. After that I started to draw rough sketches and then I began using water colours.

'I could get over my grief while I was drawing pictures, I could forget my life without arms.'

Nevertheless Iwao suffered from deep depression when not working on the scraps of paper he saved.

'I hated to be called Daruma – man without hands – and have stones thrown at me, so I exercised secretly at night. This later bore fruit when in the Paraplegic Games held at Yoyogi, Tokyo, I won the gold medal in the 50-metre breaststroke and a bronze medal in the stand broad jump. People said that it was great – maybe, but the work that had led up to it was for surviving.'

After this Iwao moved to his father's apartment room which was vacant most of the time and he found it necessary to earn money to support himself. To this end he tried a variety of jobs, from baby-sitting to cleaning a cinema.

'People were unwilling to employ me because I did not have arms, and often I worked without payment to prove that I was capable of doing a job,' he says. 'And I was thankful if someone gave me work but once I was hired I was always anxious in case I should be fired – I often was and ran back home with abuse shouted after me. At one stage, when I was seventeen years old, it seemed that everything was too hard to bear and I decided I could not go on. I stood on a railway track and waited while the train came towards me with a deafening roar. At the last moment some instinct made me leap to one side.'

Two years later Iwao found regular work with the Izumiya Industries Company which manufactured road-making equipment. Being able to ride a bicycle 'no hands' he was used as a messenger at a fraction of what an able-bodied worker earned but he was delighted to be in work.

'My daily allowance was 30 yen,' he explains. 'A stuffed sweet bread called "anpan" cost 10 yen and a serving of instant noodle soup 15 yen. I did not have breakfast but at lunch time I had the bread and a glass of water, and the noodle soup for supper. Thus I was able to save five yen a day.

'Although I earned less salary I worked two or three times harder than ordinary people which was good for the employer – and good for me because through work I gained self confidence.'

It was now his ambition to try painting with oils and on 24 April 1962 – a date that is fixed in his memory – he was able to buy a set of oil colours with the money he had saved at the rate of five yen a day. As there was not enough for him to buy a palette he solved the problem by using the glass which he removed from his window after putting on all his clothing against the freezing cold of the winter nights.

In November of the same year Iwao entered an oil painting for showing in a Fuse city exhibition and not only was it accepted but was sold for the seemingly astronomical sum of 6,000 yen.

'This success overpaid me for all my efforts.' Iwao recalls. ' I wanted to throw both my arms up to the sky – instead I turned a couple of somersaults. I spent 1000 yen on colours and canvasses and donated the rest to institutions for the handicapped. People said I was so poor I should have kept all the money for myself but it just seemed too much for me.'

Iwao's gesture proved the parable of bread cast upon the waters. A newspaper ran a story on how a mouth-painting artist had given away most of the money he had earned from his first sale, and the story was picked up by the Association of Mouth and Foot Painting Artists who get to hear of so many of their members through the Press. Iwao was enrolled as a student and paid a monthly stipend which came just at the right moment as the company where he worked went bankrupt. Two years later, in 1965, he became a full member of the Association and his financial future was assured. Now Iwao was able to paint as he had always wished and he went from success to success with frequent exhibitions. He continued to work with the same determination that he had shown in learning to dress himself or proving that he was capable of working even in a humble capacity.

The extent of this success, and his remarkable output, can be gauged by this news story that in 1978 appeared in the *Mainichi Simbun*: 'The charity exhibition held by Mr Adachi, the artist without arms, on 23 and 24 of September met with great public response... He was worried whether his works would attract customers but on the first day 300 people waited for the opening at 10 o'clock and 130 works were bought before noon. The pictures he produced on the spot as a demonstration were also sold... In two days all 300 works were sold and towards the last it was became necessary to decide the buyers by drawing lots. Mr Adachi donated...1,047,000 yen to the Higashi Osaka Goodwill Bank for the welfare of the disabled.'

'There is a saying "The world is as kind as it is cruel",' says Iwao and then proceeds to tell the story of the unusual way he met his wife at the end of 1969. In the autumn of that year he returned home from sketching Lake Biwa for a picture he wanted to enter in an exhibition. A newspaper reported how after it won a prize Iwao had presented it to an institution known as the Blue Sky Special School and as a result was inundated with letters from readers.

'It was hard work writing answers to all of them,' says Iwao, 'and for some unknown reason I left one unanswered. It was from a woman named Shoko Hidaka who came from Kyushi Miyazaki and worked in a beauty parlour. I felt very sorry that I had left her out so I found her telephone number and dialled her.

'"Hello, is that Miss Hidaka?" I asked and she replied, "Ah, you are Mr Adachi." I was surprised that she knew it was me when I phoned her for the first time but from then on we had telephone conversations and exchanged letters.

'One day she phoned me and said, "Please take me somewhere this Monday."

'"How about Nara Park?" I suggested and as we had never met we described ourselves and arranged to meet on the platform of Truruhashi Station. Next Monday in the park I learned her life story and we had long conversations until we came to the temple of the great statue of Buddha where we both offered prayers.

'The next evening Shoko rang me up, and I thought it would be to thank me for the outing. But it was certainly not that. From the other end of the line came the words "If you think it would be good for you, please make me your bride. I have just phoned my mother in Kyushu and she agrees. So please marry me.

'Later I learned what she had asked of the Buddha – "I should like to live with this disabled person so please make it come true. I know hardships might lie ahead for me but that's OK."

'The great Buddha statue responded beautifully. Maybe I was not disabled in my heart and Shoko became my wife.'

In January 1970 the marriage of Iwao and Shoko was registered and towards the end of the year she gave birth to a baby girl they named Emiko – the daughter whom Iwao declared 'gives me the energy for tomorrow.'

Johnny Ang

'No regret, no anger, no self-pity.'

It was the end of the day and for the man watching the sun sink below the rim of the world it was a time for reflection. Waves tinged with the flush of sunset rolled in from the South China Sea and hissed up the white sand of Johor Baru, almost reaching the wheelchair of the silent watcher. For him the return to this lonely, tranquil spot was an act of faith. In his mind's eye he saw the beach in bright sunlight as it had been years ago – the 4th of October 1959, to be exact – when as an exuberant youth of eighteen he had come here with a swimming party.

'Let me get a photo of you diving off that jetty,' shouted a friend. Though reluctant Johnny Ang finally responded to the repeated request but as he dived he was distracted by the camera and twisted his head. The impact of striking the water in this position damaged his spine so severely that only two of his vertebrae continued to function.

'I was rushed to the Sultanah Aminah General Hospital nearby,' Johnny was to recall later. 'However, owing to a lack of adequate medical facilities there, my friends decided to transfer me to Singapore. But I was hijacked on the way to the Singapore General Hospital and ended up at home instead. Unbeknown to me there was a big disagreement between my young companions and the older generation of family friends as to the most effective means of treatment. The older generation had their way and I was attended by a Chinese physician.

'All this meant extra suffering, unprofessional mishandling and unnecessary delay which aggravated my injuries. By the time I was admitted to the Singapore hospital three days after the accident, I was literally more dead than alive. Doctors were amazed that I was still living after such mistreatment. Unconsciousness was indeed a welcome relief.'

After Johnny returned to awareness he was told that he would be disabled for the rest of his life, being paralysed from the neck down.

The months and then years that followed were bitter ones for the young man who had so looked forward to an active and challenging life. The son of a hawker, Johnny had set up a chicken farm in order to put himself through school, but now his dreams had died at the Lido Beach in Johor Baru. And with them died his self-esteem and self-confidence.

'I was ashamed,' he says today. 'The self pity was overwhelming. On bad days I would even growl at the sweet nurses.'

His state of mind can be gauged by what he recently told a journalist, 'Anyone who has gone through that ordeal and says he never thought of killing himself is a liar.'

After two years in hospital Johnny was transferred to the Mount Alvernia Hospital run by the nuns of the Franciscan Mission of Divine Motherhood.

'Given the security and imbued with new-found faith as a Catholic after five years in Mount Alvernia, I was able to gather together the shattered pieces of my life,' Johnny says. 'After having groped through a period in the darkness of ignorance and despair, not knowing where to turn, I accidently stumbled on to the path along which I have meandered since.'

One day a nurse placed Johnny's transistor radio at his side. It was at a time he was consumed with frustration and using the slight movement left in his right arm he pushed his wrist on the tuning knob with unreasoning force, accidently tuning in to a relay of the World Service.

Reliving that moment Johnny says, 'Suddenly the quiet was shattered. "...an electric typewriter which can be operated by a person with total paralysis – that's to say someone who can't move their limbs, trunk or head. Here to tell you about this remarkable invention is Dr W. A. R. Thomson..." It was a voice from Heaven, a voice of hope, a voice of salvation! Yes, it was the voice for which I had waited for years.'

The equipment Dr Thomson described in the broadcast was known as the Possum, from the initials POSM*, a machine that allowed quadriplegics to operate special equipment by blowing down a tube. Johnny became the first Possum-user in Asia and, as the apparatus enabled him to type, he took courses in journalism and short-story writing. In the first lesson of the latter course he wrote a short story entitled 'Every Rose Hides a Thorn' and – to Johnny's amazement and delight – it was published in *Her World*, a popular women's magazine in Singapore and Malaysia.

[Today Johnny Ang is the editor of the bi-monthly *Handicaps' Digest*, the publication of the Handicaps Welfare Association which exists to foster the idea of self-help and mutual assistance among the disabled.]

It was Erich Krell, the Australian mouth painter, who encouraged Johnny to try painting when on a visit to Singapore in 1988. Already Johnny was accustomed to using a mouthstick to operate a computer and now he attempted to replace it with a brush.

His feelings about this new venture are summed up in these extracts from a letter he wrote to Erich Krell in March 1989: 'Since you have taken so much trouble and suffering to kick me on the butt to get started on mouth-painting, I knew I had to try. Nobody ever pushed me as hard as you have done. Nobody has so much faith that I have the ability to paint... in fact I had looked for excuses and procrastinated in the hope that I wouldn't have to face up to it. I was scared stiff but when you threatened to break off the friendship if I didn't give it a try, I knew the day of reckoning wasn't far away. When I promised you before you left Singapore that I would begin in the New Year – I did. The pictures enclosed are the proof!'

Johnny went on to explain that he had not painted a stroke in his life, indeed he had not even written a letter of the alphabet during the past thirty years. Now his first painting was entitled 'The Birthday Rabbit' and he said in his letter: 'After painting the Rabbit, it took me a full day to realize that it wasn't a lucky coincidence. Perhaps I could draw after all. The fear disappeared. I concentrated and focused my energy and drew upon whatever hidden artistic talent I might have. Each subsequent painting gave me more confidence and increased my enthusiasm. I am now committed.'

In September of the same year Johnny was accepted as a student by the Association of Mouth and Foot Painting Artists.

Let us return to the white beach at Johor Baru and the man watching the sun set over the scene of his accident so many years ago. Here had ended so much hope, here had begun so much pain and depression but memories of this were interspersed with a sense of achievement and acceptance.

As the sun finally sank out of sight Johnny Ang said to the friend who had driven him out to this spot, 'No regret, no anger, no self-pity.'

Many a good story ends with a sunset but in Johnny's case there is much more to tell. His painting has progressed to a point where in 1993 the Singapore Mint selected one of his works as the subject for silver and gold medallions. The picture is entitled 'Carps in a Lily Pond' and the medallions commemorate the tenth anniversary of the Singapore Community Chest which helps voluntary welfare organisations.

*Patient Operated Selector Mechanism

The same year Johnny received an accolade that once would have seemed beyond belief – he was presented with the International Victory Award. This award, in recognition of disabled people who show exceptional courage and are role models for others, is sponsored by the National Rehabilitation Hospital in Washington DC and previously had only been bestowed upon Americans.

In paying tribute to Johnny the Prime Minister of Singapore, Mr Goh Chok Tong, declared 'I know him personally. He was my schoolmate in Raffles Institution. I also taught for a while in the same Chinese primary school where he taught when he had the accident. Today he is an accomplished essayist and mouth artist.'

In April 1993 Johnny had an adventurous time in travelling to the USA to collect his award. First stop was London where he stayed with his niece Doreen and her husband Stephen Bird in the Barbican.

'On 24th of April, at 1023 hours, there was an earth-shattering boom,' Johnny recalls. 'Right before my eyes, barely three hundred metres away, a mushroom cloud of black smoke enveloped the Hong Kong Bank building. When the smoke cleared many minutes later it was a ruin. The newly repaired NatWest Tower next to it suffered the same fate. The IRA had done it again to NatWest! The buildings along the street were shattered and we were greatly inconvenienced as we were living within the cordoned-off security area.

'Worse was to come. The next day at Heathrow Airport British Airways refused to fly us – everyone responsible, including BA in Singapore, the ticket agents and myself, had forgotten about visas to enter the US. With Stephen's help and though frantic calls on a Sunday to the American Embassy in London, the Singapore Embassy in Washington and the organising co-ordinator at the National Rehabilitation Hospital, we finally managed to get an assurance that visas would be waiting for us at Dulles International Airport.

'We managed to catch the last flight to Washington with only minutes to spare. On arrival our Singapore Ambassador, Mr S. R. Nathan, met us inside the airport security area to make sure we got through Immigration.'

The result was that Johnny was just in time for the Gala Presentation and Ceremony, and this was followed by a Congressional Breakfast with Senators and Congressmen and a visit to the White House for a meeting with the Vice-President Mr Al Gore.

Today life continues to be full for Johnny. His enthusiasm for painting is undiminished despite an increasing difficulty resulting from cervical spondylosis which is literally a pain in the neck. Because of this pain he can only paint for a period of only two to three hours, and because his movement is limited he can only cover an area of 25 sq. cm. at a time so, as he puts it, his painting is put together like a jigsaw puzzle.

'Now I have only one ambition left,' he declares. 'And that is to be accepted as a full member of the MFPA before I reach my grave.'

Eros Bonamini

'I have all the interests of ordinary mortals.'

'Ihave known very few artists of of such clear intelligence and equally vivacious irony. For the past twenty years he (Eros Bonamini) has continued to develop, constantly and coherently, his research, not for anything worried by finding himself out of step with certain of today's artistic expressions.'

So wrote art critic Eugenio Miccini in an introduction to a book entitled *Cronotopografie* which covers nineteen years of Eros Bonamini's experiments in art. This well illustrated work gives an indication of the versatility of an artist who on one hand strives to proclaim his ideas in highly abstract art and on the other can paint realistic still lifes and landscapes. His work, that some would call avant garde, is an example of how members of the Association of Mouth and Foot Painters develop their own styles – there are over four hundred such artists in the world and they have over four hundred approaches to art.

Eros Bonamini was born in Verona in 1942. As he grew up he studied technical subjects at school and had a great love of mathematics, and it is doubtful that it ever crossed his mind that one day he would become a professional painter. But whatever plans he had for his future ended abruptly in one day in 1960.

Although not a dedicated sportsman, Eros enjoyed games and swimming and diving, and, as with a number of other AMFPA members, it was a diving accident that caused him to be paralysed from the neck down. When he recovered enough from his ordeal he returned home where he was was confined to a wheelchair.

'After the accident I often found myself alone and with a great deal of time to think,' he told the author. 'To pass the time I threw myself into literature and specialized in certain fields. Then by chance I discovered painting which opened up an entirely new vista for me. Since then I have dedicated myself entirely to painting.'

From the moment he first had the handle of a paint brush positioned between his teeth, Eros developed his latent talent at a remarkable rate. The director of a publishing house in Verona became interested when he heard of the young man who was painting by means of his mouth and visited his home. He was highly impressed by the work he saw and introduced it to the AMFPA. In March 1966 Eros became a member and later was to be voted on to the Board of the Association.

Although Eros began as a pictorial painter, his lively mind began considering the more abstract elements of art, especially Cubism. This artistic movement owed its origins to Picasso and Braque in 1907 and it rapidly influenced Western painting. In Cubism the artist divided the subject of the picture into a number of parts and depicted differing aspects of it on the same canvas. Later Picasso added to the genre by cutting up pieces of newspaper which he included in his pictures.

'Cubism has interested me because it is an operation on Time,' Eros explains, 'made up of a simultaneity of the artist's points of view so that an object and a landscape presented simultaneously on the same canvas shows a complex reality. And this was perhaps the start of my particular work on Time – I should say, of my curiosity on the operation of Time.'

Perhaps it was his early study of mathematics that inspired Eros to explore the nature of Time through the medium of art. But such an exploration could not be undertaken with conventional paint and canvas, the artist devised his own materials to undertake the quest which is charted in the book *Cronotopografie*.

An idea how Eros developed his materials and technique can be gathered from an article by the critic Alberto Veca in which he explained that cement and adhesive were first treated as 'pigment'.

'Then Bonamini enquired into the hardening process of the material,' he wrote, 'working on it with an incision of constant form and pressure: the outcome was a succession of scratches which tended to disappear as the drying process was completed. The variation of the adhesives signified a different behaviour on the part of the material: a matter of wishing to associate the constant differentiated reaction of the cement in the face of the same aggressive process.

'This was the reasoning on the "relativity" of the means and on the outcome which was accepted on its merits as a direct and true testimony of the working process. One must, together with this, look at a further enquiry made by Bonamini into materials in about 1977 when the scratch on the cement was replaced by ribbons of canvas soaked in different strengths of peroxide and, successively, placed in ink for a constant time. The result – each strip corresponds to a specific degree of absorption of the ink – becomes part of a sequence in which the various elements are displayed in succession, evidencing in its horizontal layout, the diversity of the physical results in the presence of the identity of the gestures.'

To those not familiar with the language of abstract art the above may seem rather esoteric but art depends on innovation if it is not to decline and the great artists of this century all added to the progress of art by experimentation. And how successful has Eros been in his development of new modes of expression related to his 'curiosity on the operation of Time'?

The answer is probably best expressed by the writer Giorgio Cortenova who, writing a catalogue for Verona's Ferrari Gallery in 1989, said: 'Following all his works over the years...I feel it fair to state that it is rare for an artist of our time to be able coherently to enrich and renew his work as does Bonamini. What is more, I cannot hide the intense feelings I have, the sensation his work gives me. How moved I was only yesterday coming out of his studio and dwelling on his work! What stands out today in his present language is the growth of a new energy...'

It is not just the words of art critics that endorse his work but the number of exhibitions in Italy and around the world in which it has appeared.

Eros Bonamini the artist is well known, Eros Bonamini the man is reserved when it comes to speaking about himself. To him it is his pictures that count and it is interesting to note that in the book *Cronotopografie*, in which various distinguished writers on art discuss his work, not a single mention is made of the fact that he is disabled.

To the author he did go so far as to say, 'I have all the interests of ordinary mortals – sometimes more important, sometimes less important. I love to travel a lot, I love many things... I am married and my wife is called Giuseppina – at home we call her "Giusi" – and my parents live in their own house not far from our home.

'I have no religious conviction though I have a religious culture having been educated in a certain way. But I am very logical, absolutely logical. And to someone who has had my kind of experience in life I would say that culture is an option and can become a reason for living.'

Kun-Shan Hsieh

'A special touch of humanity.'

'I owe so much to the loving care of my mother.' These words have been repeated over and over by Kun-Shan Hsieh when giving interviews to journalists about his art and life. Yet no matter how many times this phrase has been quoted it never loses its sincerity as far as Kun-Shan is concerned. He can never forget that after his accident a number of his relatives and family friends were full of suggestions as to how his parents could rid themselves of the liability of a severely disabled son. His mother's response was to insist on being with him no matter what the future held.

Inspired by her love and devotion, Kun-Shan was determined to defy all the odds against him and not let her down.

Kun-Shan was born in Taitung in eastern Taiwan in 1958. His parents were poor peasants but their economic situation - five family members shared a tiny apartment - in no way prevented the boy from enjoying a happy childhood. In due course he attended an elementary school and when he completed his basic education he regarded himself as lucky when he was taken on as a worker in a garment factory.

In 1972 word spread among the staff that they were going to be relocated in a new factory, and in February of the following year the move to the new site began. Fifteen-year-old Kun-Shan was excited by the prospect and enthusiastically joined in the work of removing machinery from the old plant. It was a break in the rather dull routine of factory life and the youth was in high spirits as he helped to load a truck. Grasping a piece of metal he raised it high to place it on top of the pile forgetting how high he was above the ground...

The metal touched a high voltage cable overhead and a devastating burst of electricity surged through it and the youth who was holding it. Kun-Shan was rushed to hospital where in order to save his life doctors carried out drastic surgery. When he finally recovered consciousness it was to find that his entire left arm had been amputated as had three-quarters of his right arm and his right leg at the knee.

No wonder friends of the Hsieh family shook their heads - a youth with only one limb left would be a terrible burden on those who were already hard pressed in the struggle for existence. There must be ways in which this responsibility could be shed...

And it was at this point that Kun-Shan's mother declared her devotion to her disabled son - at the time it was the only ray of light in his darkened world. In those days there was no sophisticated equipment or training programmes to help someone so handicapped, no computers that could be worked with a mouthstick or electric wheelchairs that could be controlled electronically through the movement of the patient's chin.

Months passed as Kun-Shan slowly recovered from the surgery he had undergone and he continually asked himself what could the future hold for someone who had lost the use of their body. And as the months became years the question remained unanswered.

It was in 1980 that this maimed garment-worker discovered the creative pleasure of painting. Before then he had passed the time by endeavouring to draw simple sketches with a pencil held between his teeth, and then one day he tried 'doodling' with a paintbrush.

'Suddenly I entered a world of my own,' he explains. 'All the loneliness, frustration and pain disappeared when I was painting.'

There is a long way to go between doodling and producing an actual painting but having discovered his new world Kun-Shan was determined to make the journey. At the beginning he practised for ten hours a day to get the necessary control. Sometimes he was so exhausted that he would fall asleep in front of his picture.

'Painting was so much on my mind that sometimes I would wake up with a start and immediately begin to add a few strokes on an unfinished canvas,' he says.

When he felt confident that he could use a brush in this way he attended art classes to learn the essentials of what was to be his unexpected profession. As his technique improved word began to spread about this young artist and in 1985, when he held his first one-man exhibition in Taipei, the leading Taiwanese artist Shiuan-shan Wu told the Press, 'He is fast becoming one of the best in his generation. There is a special touch of humanity in his paintings.'

Reuters' correspondent covered the exhibition for the media outside Taiwan with the result that an article about Kun-Shan appeared in the *Reader's Digest*.

'In a country still primarily interested in Chinese watercolours and calligraphy, Hsieh's paintings have created a new interest in oils,' the *Digest* declared. It also quoted Chau-chu Ho, a committee member of the Taiwan Oil Painting Association, who in speaking of Kun-Shan, stated, 'He has set an example to all the handicapped that they are not a burden on society but rather a creative force if they are given the chance.'

The Taipei exhibition was a great success not only because all the thirty-two paintings exhibited found buyers but also because the Press report led to the Association of Mouth and Foot Painting Artists contacting Kun-Shan through the gallery where his exhibition had been held. The same year he was invited to join the organisation.

Since then Kun-Shan's reputation as an artist has continued to grow. What is intriguing about his work is the fact that he is at ease with both European and traditional Chinese techniques. His favourite motifs are flowers and animals and an example of his typical traditional work shows a pair of birds with bright plumage amid the most delicately tinted blooms. Another picture with a European influence depicts flowers in blue flower pots painted with bold impressionistic strokes in gaudy colours that seem to radiate sunshine and heat. It seems remarkable that two such differing paintings could be the work of the same artist.

In speaking about his work he declares that he still wants to learn more about painting and that it is his aim to establish a unique style of his own which will reflect in his works.

Apart from giving Kun-Shan a profession, his involvement in art led indirectly to the happiest aspect of his life. In 1980, when his interest in painting had begun to change his life, he visited a friend at his studio near Taipei. Here he met a charming girl named Su-Fen Line and was greatly attracted by her. In 1987 they married and today they have two daughters, Ning who was born in 1989 and Hsuen who was born in 1992. One of Kun-Shan's delights is to go swimming with his daughters.

Apart from painting and his family, his greatest enjoyment is in travel and his other interests include Chinese chess, watching ball games and singing - a full life for one who once it seemed had nothing to look forward to.

Nancy Rae Litteral

'Disabled does not mean unable.'

The year 1954 began as a very good year for high school student Nancy Rae Litteral in the small town of Wheelersburg in the American Mid-West. 'I was seventeen and it was a very exciting age for me,' she says today. 'The High School Sextet was kept busy singing, especially since we'd returned from New York where we'd won second place on the televised Ted Mack Amateur Hour. Soon graduation, then college.

'I had enjoyed an ideal childhood along with an older sister, Anna Lou, and two younger brothers, Robert and David. With mother we attended the Wheelersburg Baptist Church, and Anna Lou and I were now very excited about going to the same Christian college in the fall. Our whole life was ahead of us – we felt blessed.

'May 4 had been a lovely warm day. The Sextet was singing during intermission of the Senior class play. When the performance was over I prepared to walk home as our car was in the garage for repairs but friends offered me a ride home. On the way we were hit head on by a drunken driver. The next thing I knew I was lying on the floor without movement or feeling. Later the hospital X-rays showed that my neck was broken.'

The doctors offered no hope of recovery to Nancy's stricken family who took turns at staying with her.

One night she asked her father to read her the 23rd Psalm. He had been religious as a young man but now he no longer attended the church. When he finished with the words '...and I will dwell in the house of the Lord for ever,' Nancy asked, 'Daddy, if I die will I see you in Heaven?'

Ray Litteral could find no reply, in silence he left the room. Nancy asked a nurse to call her pastor and to her joy 'that night Daddy rededicated his life to the Lord – our prayers were answered,' as she recalled later.

After nine weeks the doctors broke it to Nancy's parents that she would never get any movement or feeling back, she would remain paralysed from the neck down, and as there was nothing further that could be done in hospital she would probably be happier in her home surroundings.

'So I went home, watched television and cried,' she says. 'God hadn't answered our prayers and my life seemed ended. Instead of going off to college, here I was totally helpless with my parents taking care of me like a baby. I was full of self pity and questioning God, "Why me?"'

This unhappy period ended when it was arranged for Nancy to go to Ohio State University Hospital for a year of rehabilitation. Here she met other quadriplegics and out of their mutual encouragement came laughter. Occupational therapists made a device that enabled Nancy to hold a pen in her right hand, the only part of her body that retained a little movement. Now she learned to write again and as something to pass the time began 'painting by numbers', putting colour into outlined spaces in order to build up a picture.

This was Nancy's introduction to painting. At school she was so 'unartistic' that she would bribe a schoolmate to do her art class drawings for her at fifty cents a time. Now to her amazement she found that she not only enjoyed painting but actually seemed to have a talent for it.

When Nancy returned home she found that certain Bible verses gave her support. One such verse was Philippians 4:13 'I can do all things through Christ which strengtheneth me.'

'This verse showed me that I could live a life of paralysis for the rest of my life with Christ's help,' Nancy declares. 'I was fortunate to have such dedicated parents who sacrificed so much to care for me. We settled into a daily routine. After my mother and father got me up in my wheelchair I'd paint until my arm got tired, then would read, type – using a mouth-held stick to hit the keys – and watch a little television before going to bed at eleven. We did this every day except Sunday when we went to church, and this is still my routine.'

After a while Nancy grew tired of painting by numbers. The pastime had played its part in developing her ability to use a brush and apply paint but now she wanted to be more creative and to this end in 1960 she enrolled in a correspondence art course at which she worked with great dedication for the next three years. Her reward came when she actually began to sell her paintings.

Meanwhile her sister and brothers married and had their families. Her brother Robert with his wife and two children embarked on missionary work in Papua, New Guinea, and her brother David went into the family grocery business with her father – their store is named the Nancy Rae Supermarket and its walls are decorated with Nancy's paintings. Sister Anna Lou married an army officer, and when he was posted to Vietnam in 1967 she returned to Wheelersburg with her three young sons. Her helpful presence brought great happiness to Nancy and her parents.

A wholehearted Christian, Anna Lou showed Nancy a page in her Bible one day and asked, 'Have you seen this?'

It was a verse from I. Thessalonians 5:8 and Nancy read, 'In everything give thanks; for this is the will of God in Christ Jesus concerning you.'

'Anna Lou told me this was God's will for my life and asked if I'd ever given thanks for it,' says Nancy. 'This verse gave me real joy and a different outlook on my handicap.'

But this joy was soon to be tempered with sorrow. It was a warm cloudy day in Ohio on 23 April 1968. Anna Lou visited her brother David and was in his house when it was completely destroyed by a tornado. David's wife and Anna Lou were injured, and three days later Anna Lou died along with three other victims.

'We were heartbroken and some people in the town could not understand all the tragedy that had happened to our family and felt it didn't pay to live a Christian life,' Nancy says. 'But they just didn't understand that our lives are in God's hands.'

Arthritis brought an end to Nancy's painting with a brush taped to her hand, and so she began to work with a brush held in her mouth. One of the problems that beset mouth painters is the effect of having to clench a brush handle hard between their teeth, but in Nancy's case a dentist designed a holder that protected her teeth and allowed her to paint for hours at a stretch. She also uses paint brushes with magnetic handles which enable her to change them in the mouthpiece without having to call upon her mother for help

Her favourite subjects were flowers, still life and especially studies of children, and there is an obvious relationship between this and a remark Nancy made in a magazine interview, 'What I miss the most is to take a child into my arms.'

One day in 1979 Nancy was fascinated to read in a copy of *Reader's Digest* an article on the Association of Mouth and Foot Painting Artists, the American partnership affiliated to it being called the Association of Handicapped Artists. She submitted some of her paintings to the Association but the reply was that the board did not consider her to be qualified for a scholarship.

Undeterred she submitted more paintings the following year with the result that she was accepted as a student.

MYRON ANGUS
Plum Point
Watercolour   30 x 23 cm

MYRON ANGUS   *Springtime by the Coast*   Watercolour   28 x 38 cm

IWAO ADACHI
In the Jungle
Oil

Opposite: IWAO ADACHI
Rothenburg, Romantic Street
Oil   82 x 53 cm

IWAO ADACHI   *In the Countryside* Oil   61 x 72 cm

JOHNNY ANG
Kingfisher
Acrylic   30 x 41 cm

JOHNNY ANG   *In Search of Home*   Acrylic   41 x 51 cm

156

EROS BONAMINI *Sounding Venezia* Collage

EROS BONAMINI *Market in Morocco* Oil 55 x 45 cm

Overleaf: EROS BONAMINI
Harbour Venere
Oil 50 x 70 cm

157

KUN-SHAN HSIEH
Flower Still Life with Bird and Insects
Watercolour   75 x 40 cm

KUN-SHAN HSIEH *Still Life* Watercolour   60 x 89 cm

160

KUN-SHAN HSIEH *Girl with a red Pillow* Oil 52 x 41 cm

Overleaf: KUN-SHAN HSIEH
Flower Still Life
Oil 90 x 115 cm

NANCY RAE LITTERAL
Picking Daisies
Oil   50 x 40 cm

NANCY RAE LITTERAL   *At the Sea*   Oil   21 x 25 cm

NANCY RAE LITTERAL *Flower Still Life* Oil 40 x 30 cm

JINGSHENG LIU
Peonies in a Vase
Watercolour   69 x 45 cm

JINGSHENG LIU
Two Little Cats
Tusche   68 x 44 cm

SOON YI OH *Summer* Watercolour   48 x 44 cm

SOON YI OH
Mountain Landscape with Waterfall
Ink/Watercolour   56 x 57 cm

167

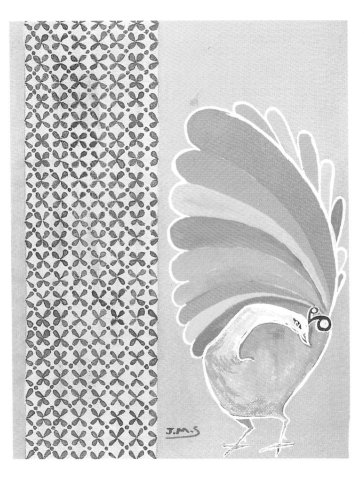

JAYANTILAL SHIHORA
Peacock
Tempera   29 x 19 cm

JAYANTILAL SHIHORA
Tree with Birds
Tempera   27 x 19 cm

In 1991 Nancy became a full member of the Association and her work in the form of greetings cards has been appreciated in many parts of the world.

Apart from work for the Association, Nancy accepts commissions and much of her income from this is passed on to charities and her missionary brother to be used for the welfare of children. She told the author, 'I have an art show once a year and I enter my paintings in the county fair but most commissions come through word of mouth. People come to the house with photographs of what they want painted. I've painted helicopters, boats, cars, dogs and cats, and of course portraits of people's loved ones. Right now I am painting a picture of a wedding. But as well as this work I paint what I want to paint for the Association.

'Painting gives me much pleasure and a feeling of accomplishment. Disabled does not mean unable. We handicapped must not dwell on the things we cannot do but focus on the many things we can. God has been good to me and blessed me with a wonderful supportive family, church and friends. I couldn't have made it without God's love or their help.'

Jingsheng Liu

'An ardent love for life'

To begin with it was just another routine day in May 1978 at the Beijing 5 Paper Mill, then alarming news spread from department to department. In hushed voices workers passed on the word that somebody had been hurt... it had been caused by an electrical fault... the victim was an electrician well known because he had been with the company since 1969... he had been rushed to hospital... there was little hope...

In the Beijing hospital surgeons declared that the only way to save the life of Jingsheng Liu was to amputate his arms which had taken the full force of high voltage electrical discharge. When the young man came round from the operation it was to find that he had lost each arm at the shoulder.

'When I recovered to face a miserable fate I was completely lost ,' Jingsheng admits. 'For a time I was plunged into despair. I was then twenty-six years old and I felt great sorrow at the thought of the long years ahead but I knew that I had to face the challenge caused by this sudden change in my life.'

Jingsheng's workmates at the paper mill did not forget him and were generous with their help, and it depressed the house-bound invalid that he was unable to express his gratitude for their concern. One day an idea occurred to him and he asked members of his family to place a pen between his toes and then, lying prone on his bed, he managed to write four Chinese characters which read 'Thank you all.'

Little did Jingsheng know it but this was the first step to a new life. At the time he merely saw the mouth-held pen as a way of escaping the frustration of home-bound disability.

An inner voice told him: If you could write then you would be able to work.

'So I began trying to write with my toes,' Jingsheng recalls. 'Soon I found this was not a convenient way of writing so I changed to holding the writing brush with my mouth and I worked very hard to master this skill. Yet for a long time I found it was not a comfortable way to write as it brought on dizziness as well as mouth problems so I tried a third way of writing by moving my shoulders.

'I designed a metal frame to be strapped to the shoulder with a handle to grip the brushes used for Chinese lettering. After long and tedious months practise I began to master my "iron arm".'

Later he returned to the mouth-held brush as he progressed into more delicate calligraphy and then painting.

Jingsheng was encouraged in his self-imposed rehabilitation by the fact that in 1979 he married a young woman named Mao Dahua who, in Jingsheng's words, 'was willing to look after her armless husband for life.'

Exactly two years after his accident Jingsheng returned to work at the paper mill as a librarian. He had worked so intensely to master the skill of writing characters that his interest in their form was aroused and he began to study calligraphy – the art of fine writing.

'Working in the library I thought more and more about disabled people like me and that they could and should live the same as ordinary people with equal rights and responsibilities,' says Jingsheng. 'In order to help them I realised I had to improve myself and to this end I began to train myself in the field of Chinese literature and calligraphy with the help of a correspondence course. In 1983 I received my certificate from the Correspondence University and I became a member of the Beijing Calligraphers Association.'

A definition of calligraphy is 'free hand writing in which the freedom is so nicely reconciled with order that the understanding eye is pleased to contemplate it.' And Jingsheng, like other calligraphers, saw there can be beauty in the way characters are formed and in their relationship to each other. To him the delicate art use of the lettering brush produced much more than mere neat writing – it was an art form. Soon his work was to be seen in exhibitions not only in China but in Japan and Hong Kong.

According to Jingsheng his real artistic life began in 1987.

'At the beginning of that year a German, Mr Ohlmer who was the Far Eastern representative of the AMFPA and who had devoted his life to the cause of the disabled, read an article about me in China Reconstruction and decided to make a long journey to China to visit me.' Jingsheng explains, 'We had great talks about philosophy, literature and art and he asked me, "From which university did you graduate?" When I shook my head and explained that I had not had such an education he said, "You are more like a scholar than a worker." I replied, "For this perhaps I must thank fate."

'Through Mr Ohlmer's introduction I was admitted to AMFPA as the first recruit from mainland China. I was happy to receive such an honour and at the time I decided to broaden my interest in Chinese painting.'

Thanks to the stipend provided by the Association Jingsheng was able to spend three years in the Chinese Painting Department of the Special Education College of Changchun University. After graduating in 1990 he worked in the Huaxai Calligraphy and Painting Society and from then on his career as both a calligrapher and artist accelerated. In that year he visited the United States as a representative of Chinese disabled university students and participated in a painting exhibition held in the United Nations Mansion and at the Kennedy Centre — Jingsheng had come a very long way from the days when he sat at home and wondered gloomily what the future could hold for someone who had lost their arms.

Since his visit to America Jingsheng has had his paintings displayed in various exhibitions including one organised by the AMFPA in Taiwan, while in 1993 his works were included in the China Handicapped Calligraphy and Painting Exhibition held in the Sun Arts Gallery of Japan and here he won the top prize of the exhibition.

But with success Jingsheng had not forgotten the concern for the handicapped which inspired him when he was a librarian at his old paper mill – today he is Vice-President of the Beijing Organisation of Physically Handicapped Artists. And somehow he finds time to be a member of his district parliament.

'What I have achieved is due to the support of my family, and I am most grateful to my wife who does all my "arm work" in daily life,' Jingsheng says. 'She has brought up our only son who is now in his teens and she was my assistant during my art training.'

And speaking about his artistic work Jingsheng continues, 'The type of my Chinese calligraphy and painting can be traced to the influence of Chinese traditional artistic masterpieces. My calligraphy is best presented in the style known as "Xing-Shu" while my paintings are mostly about flowers and birds. What I like is a special effect that is produced when colours, water and Chinese ink come into contact with the special paper called "Xhan Zhi" through my paint brush.

'What I seek through my creative works can be summarised as simplicity, originality and an ardent love for life.'

Soon-Yi Oh

'Anguish and patience'

It was a hot summer's day in South Korea when three-year-old Soon-Yi Oh went to bathe in a river that flowed opposite her home in MaSan City. The little girl felt secure because she was with half a dozen children who were four or five years older than herself, and they would see that she came to no harm in the water. Added to her sense of security was the fact that she could see her parents' house beyond the railway line that ran beside the river bank.

For a while the children played at the water's edge, laughing and splashing until they decided that it was time to leave the river. Still laughing they raced up the bank with Soon-Yi bravely toddling after them. They had just reached the railway tracks when a locomotive came into view...

Mercifully Soon-Yi has no recollection of what happened next, of how the older children were able to scatter to safety but at three she was not nimble enough to get clear. She was struck by the on-coming engine and both her arms were amputated. What she does remember is that the following years were very miserable ones.

Born in 1966, Soon-Yi had two brothers and two sisters in what she describes as 'an ordinary family', her father being a carpenter. Looking back on her early life she says, 'There are many people who have an influence on me, among them my family, teachers and friends who were concerned about my education, especially in the fine arts.'

Despite the pain and frustration that she suffered after her accident, by the age of five Soon-Yi was able to use her foot for everyday tasks almost with the same dexterity that able-bodied children use their hands. She attended primary school and it was in her fourth year there that her teacher suggested she should try painting with a brush held between her toes.

The effect this had on the ten-year-old was profound.

'I am sure I was destined to work in an artistic field whether I was to be handicapped or not,' she declares. 'I have painted every day since the age of ten.' The fact that she felt she had found her metier through brush and canvas did not mean that foot painting came to her easily.

'I learned painting with difficulty,' she says. 'I learned with a mixture of anguish and patience. Although it was a time of suffering, once I started learning to paint I could not get the thought of art out of my mind.

'One practical advantage was that because I had used my foot as a hand from an early age I had the strength to use a brush. And when I found that I could perform an exact function such as drawing a line I was tremendously encouraged. But I still have difficulty expressing the more elaborate parts of my pictures but with effort I shall achieve greater skill.'

Soon-Yi is a perfectionist. In looking at her delicate and evocative landscapes it is hard to imagine that she has difficulty with the 'more elaborate parts'.

In 1985 when she was 19, Soon-Yi's painstaking efforts were rewarded by winning the first prize in the National High School Student's Art Contest which was sponsored by Hongik University. Television cameras presented the awards ceremony to South Korea and the carpenter's daughter who, sixteen years earlier had fallen under a train, had her first taste of fame.

The prize was not only a recognition that Soon-Yi's mouth-held brush could produce pictures that were judged ahead of her able-bodied fellows but the publicity it generated led her to being invited to become a student member of the Association of Mouth and Foot Painting Artists. This was to prove of immense help to her when she enroled at Dun Kug University to study Fine Arts.

'When I entered as a freshman I found many unexpected difficulties,' she says. 'But I received financial help from AMFPA. After graduating in 1990 I continued my studies in Taipei and then went to the graduate school of the National Academy of Fine Arts in the People's Republic of China. Here I study the history and art, art criticism and, of course, painting.'

Speaking of her work, Soon-Yi explains, 'I think a great deal and meditate before I start painting. It takes a long time for me to finish a painting and therefore I always study the challenges that it is going to present. The motifs I like to work on are from nature – landscapes and studies of four plants that I find particularly graceful – plum, orchid, chrysanthemums and bamboo – and sometimes I like to work these into abstract paintings.

'I have a great feeling of achievement when I finish a work though in my opinion the process of reaching the goal is more important, and above all what I strive for is to be faithful to myself. It is my dream to accomplish work of the finest quality.

'I had a hard time learning art but I think I have overcome the difficulties through the expression of my mind into paintings. I had to deal with blue moods and disappointments which I overcame by devoting myself to meditating, reading and above all painting.

'I always wanted to become an example to other handicapped people and to anyone who finds themselves in circumstances like mine I would say that one should collect oneself up in order to do one's best at all times with a clear mind and cultivate understanding for other people.'

Klaus Spahni

'It's the result that counts.'

From his very first memory Klaus Spahni has been in love with colour. When he was three-and-a-half years old a relative living with his family produced brushes and paints and announced that Klaus was going to help her to paint a table.

'I remember very well the powerful emotion I felt,' the artist recalls. 'Firstly to be allowed to help was so important and secondly the delight that burst forth at painting the new colour over the old. Chequered squares in different colours had to be painted precisely and this gave me a strong experience of what "coloured" meant.

'A further intensive colour-form experience occurred when I found myself in the kindergarten at the age of five. We children were given felt, little hammers, nails and pieces of wood of different basic colours and forms – round, triangular, right-angled blocks and small rods in red, yellow, blue and green. I felt such intense happiness and delight to build myself a car, a locomotive, a house that even now this early experience has stayed alive in my memory.'

Klaus Spahni was born in Willisau, Switzerland, in 1940. Until the age of nine his childhood was a happy one during which he developed the ambition to become an artist.

'When I was about seven years old I received a box of watercolour paints,' he says. 'The many paint-blocks were a wonderful collection of colours – a sight for sore eyes for someone eager to paint. To go with the set my father made me an easel out of wood remnants. As I stood there in front of my easel with painting pad, paint box, brushes and water, ready to paint my first work with the new equipment, I was overwhelmed by a feeling of importance. The sense of good fortune to be painting was coupled with the desire to carry it out like a professional.'

Two years after his father had presented him with the easel Klaus sickened and, in those days before the Salk vaccine was introduced, poliomyelitis was diagnosed, leaving him with his limbs paralysed.

When Klaus recovered from the initial ravages of the disease his father and mother took him to Zurich to be treated by a physiotherapist. Thanks to her skilled treatment the boy managed to regain the ability to sit upright, and then she inflicted – to use Klaus's word – the game of chess upon him.

To encourage the boy to attempt exercises to restore what movement he had left, the physiotherapist laid a drawing pad in front of him and squeezed a pencil between his useless fingers. A wild movement of the shoulder resulted in uncontrolled lines and circles being drawn on the paper. Klaus found this 'scribbling' fun and to try and control his gyrating hand he put his thumb in his mouth in order to steer it by movements of his head. Soon he found that he was able to draw forest settings complete with stags and scenes from the Wild West stories which he loved.

These simple mouth-and-thumb sketches gave young Klaus confidence and an enthusiasm for drawing and painting that ultimately developed into a career. Later he stopped guiding his hand by his mouth and held the pencil or brush directly between his teeth, and through this method his technique improved dramatically.

In 1955 Klaus entered a school of applied art in St Gallen and such was his enthusiasm that he had private tuition at the same time, and three years later he received instruction in scientific drawing. In 1962 he took delivery of his first electric wheelchair and enjoyed the remarkable sensation of being able to move about by himself – a liberating experience for someone who up until then had been dependant on others for his mobility. To him the best aspect of this equipment was that it allowed him to travel to sites where he wished to paint.

Nine years after he had begun his thumb-in-mouth attempts, Klaus was offered a scholarship with the Association of Mouth and Foot Painting Artists, and the following year he became a full member. With the security afforded by the Association the young painter was able to live outside his homeland in order to further his artistic studies, first in Paris and then in Spain.

In 1968 he married Kathrin Baus and the same year the couple held a joint art exhibition in the Steiger Studio Gallery in Flawil. Since then Klaus has had his paintings in many exhibitions including some which he has shared with Kathrin. Six years after their marriage the couple went to live in Spain and did not return to Switzerland until 1986. Today they live in the old university town St Gallen where Klaus continues his work.

From merely holding a pencil or brush between his teeth he has developed a method in which Kathrin tapes the implements of his profession to Japanese bamboo chopsticks. This enables him to work further back from his canvases and thus prevents fumes from the paint and varnish dissolving in his saliva and reaching his stomach with ill effects. He also finds that bamboo is light, not too hard on his teeth and has the ability to be held in the mouth for long periods without fraying.

Regarding the practical difficulties faced by mouth painters, Klaus says, 'It is naturally fascinating how people can work creatively without hands. I am constantly impressed how my foot-painting colleagues take their sure and elegant brush work for granted. The boundaries of mouth-painting lie in the length or shortness of the pencil.

'The longer the pencil, the better the eye's overview of the painting surface but the weight of the pencil becomes heavier and it follows that the lines are less secure. Conversely the shorter the pencil the closer the eye is to the canvas or paper which means less overview but the lighter the pencil the safer the stroke. The ideal range for me lies in the middle. To obtain greater mobility I use an electric wheelchair, with which I can move myself backwards and forwards, and thus can take in the picture from a distance.'

Klaus explains that ever since he can remember he has been drawn backwards and forwards between the poles of naturalistic and abstract painting – and the remarkable fact is that he is equally at home in both fields of art.

'If I paint figuratively for a while I feel the need to turn to abstraction, and vice versa,' he says. 'Both poles cross-fertilise, just as red cannot exist without green. Both impressionism and expressionism are important to impress and inspire on one hand, and on the other hand to express inner pictures and sentiments. Every creative work is a mixture of the two elements.'

Perhaps with remembrance of his childhood joy in colour in mind, Klaus declares that colour is a theme with infinite dimensions, and what fascinates him is the process of breaking into the world of colour to make discoveries and meditate upon them. His aim as a painter is that the colours 'should open themselves and openly narrate their vibrations and energies.'

Klaus has been practising mouth-painting for forty-five years and, as with the ability of a musician, he finds it a completely normal technique after years of training and what he describes as joyful practice. In stating his credo as an artist he says, 'For me, drawing and painting mean pictorial thoughts, feelings and deeds, by means of which I walk, dance, touch, run, fight, love... At the end of the day it's the result that counts – the picture, and not whether it's existence has come into being by hand, foot or mouth.'

Jayantilal Shihora

'When God closes one door...'

It was Diwali – the Hindu Festival of Lights – and fourteen-year-old Jayantilal Shihora was ducking excitedly through the crowds that filled the town of Bhavnagar in Gujarat State. Houses were illuminated with traditional oil lamps and everywhere there was the report of crackers and the lurid glare of fireworks while in the temples ceremonies were held in honour of the goddesses Lakshmi and Kali.

Suddenly Jayantilal's laughter turned to a scream as his arms were engulfed in a gush of firework flame – and in that instant his life was changed forever. He had to face a future without hands.

Jayantilal Shihora was born a normal healthy child in Bhavnagar, the son of a grain merchant.

'My father was very kind to me but in my early childhood I was deprived of maternal love when my mother died,' he explains. 'My father married again and within three years of that my elder brother died of brain fever.

'After this shock my sister married so that I was left very lonely.'

At school Jayantilal compensated for the two bereavements in his young life by dreaming of the future. He would become an engineer – or a teacher – or a doctor – at least a man with a profession. Those dreams ended with the explosion of a firework.

The following months were what Jayantilal describes as a 'dark period of depression', and when the pain of his injuries faded it was replaced with a deeper pain as he heard relatives and friends murmur, 'Without his hands there will be nothing that Jayantilal will be able to do.'

Young Jayantilal brooded on these words, particularly at night when he lay in his bed and wondered what the future could hold for someone who could not even put on his clothes or eat with a spoon. In no way could he become an engineer, a teacher, or a doctor... his past ambitions mocked him and again and again he asked himself, 'Am I a useless person?'

Then Jayantilal underwent what might be described as a mystical experience. In answer to his nightly question it seemed that he heard an inner voice. Describing it to the author he said, 'I heard words that seemed to come from a great teacher – "You have lost only your hands but not your mind or soul. They are whole." After that I felt my confidence awaken.'

From then on Jayantilal tried to do things for himself. Many times he failed but when he succeeded in performing some normally simple action, such as combing his hair or taking a bath, it was one more step on the long road to rehabilitation.

Somehow he learned to eat with a spoon despite the fact that his arms ended just below the elbows, and his greatest triumph came when he managed to ride a bicycle 'no hands'.

But though he was now less dependant on others, Jayantilal was still faced with the question: How to earn a living?

Five years after the Diwali festival misfortune a friend named Giriraj Bhartiya sent Jayantilal some postcards from Calcutta. The remarkable thing about them was that they had been painted by handicapped artists using brushes either held in their mouths or between their toes.

These greetings cards were a revelation.

'Why can't I do this?' Jayantilal asked himself. From then on he spent hours at a time with a pen clamped between his teeth endeavouring to write. At first he experienced the frustrations encountered by most disabled people when they begin the often painful task of learning to control a pen or pencil whose point is only inches away from their eyes. Things would be going well and then the line would be ruined as the pen faltered or the ache of fatigue led to disheartening results.

But Jayantilal persevered, from printing he graduated to 'joined-up' writing, and he began to manipulate a paint brush as well as a pen. Using either oils or water colours, he painted landscapes and achieved a standard so high that when he submitted his work to the Association of Mouth and Foot painting Artists he was awarded a scholarship.

'At that time I was the only Indian member,' he says. 'I was so happy and I worked harder than ever. And I remembered the saying "When God closes one door, He opens a second."'

Now that he had been granted a regular stipend Jayantilal was able to study in the Faculty of Fine Art at Baroda University. His art master Chandubhai Pandya became his guru as he not only instructed him in painting but in aspects of life that the disabled young man found to be of great value.

In 1964 Jayantilal won a first prize for art from the Lalit Kala Academy in Gujarat and from this point success followed success. The next year he received a prize for his work from the Kenny Rehabilitation Institute of Chicago and his first one-man show was held in Bombay, and since then they have been many more awards and exhibitions. The Press took up the story of the first Indian to become a member of the AMFPA and a sentence in *The Indian Express* was typical of the journalists' reaction to him – 'The painter from Bhavnagar has no hands but plenty of spirit.'

Inspired equally by European classical painters and Indian artists, Jayantilal has developed his own distinctive style.

'In the beginning I painted landscapes and sea scenes,' Jayantilal says. 'But now I concentrate on folk art using tempera colours. I love nature and like to ramble on the sea shore, in woods and on the hills and from this I seem to get strength and inspiration for creative work. I like lonely places where I feel that the natural things about me are my friends. In particular I like to sit in silence on the shore of a lake, especially at sunset which is a very special time for me.'

The year 1974 was a very special one for Jayantilal. In it he married Kiran Mehta, a Bachelor of Arts who, luckily for Jayantilal, shares his passion for nature and wandering off the beaten track.

'This was a love marriage,' he says emphatically. 'And thanks to the support Kiran gave me I have taken many steps forward with my painting. We have two sons, Sagar and Samir. Both are students, Sagar being interested in art and technology and Samir in computer studies.'

As the Festival of Diwali comes around in October or November each year Jayantilal is reminded of the accident that robbed him of his hands but none of the despair that once haunted him remains. He has found his profession as an artist and as he once told a newspaper reporter, 'I do by mouth what other artists do by their hands – there is no other difference.'

Phillip Swanepoel

'A new and purposeful life'

'I like to think of it this way – Go knew Phillip's impatience and quick-temperedness,' Cornelia Swanepoel says when talking about her husband. 'The loss of one arm first was a trial-run to see whether he would be able to cope armless.'

To the nostalgically-minded who see their children as slaves to today's electronic entertainment industry, the childhood of Phillip Swanepoel must appear idyllic, though he might not see it that way. Born in 1944, he was the youngest of a family of four and his early years were spent on a smallholding without the benefit of electricity near Randfontein, forty kilometres west of Johannesburg.

Here he gained a love of nature through rambling freely through the countryside. He also enjoyed playground sports at the school which he reached by bus – after travelling five kilometres to the gold mine from where the bus departed. When not doing his share of the household chores he built soap-box carts and somewhat reluctantly acted as 'assistant grease monkey' for his two older brothers who were forever tinkering with their old cars in order to keep them running. In short it was an active healthy life for a young boy – until early one morning in July, 1953.

'On the smallholding water had to be pumped from a borehole and it was my job on this specific morning to start the diesel pump,' Phillip recalls. 'Somehow my clothing was caught in the wheel of the pump and I was spun around. As I was slammed against the concrete floor my right arm was severed from my body. A farmworker discovered me in a pool of blood and alerted my parents.

'My father rushed me to hospital where I regained consciousness and realised my arm was gone. I remained in hospital for two weeks and started doing things with my left hand so that when I wet back to school two weeks later I could write with it. I later discovered my family, especially my mother, suffered more trauma through the accident than I did.'

Nine-year-old Phillip adapted remarkably to the loss of his limb. At school he played Rugby and soccer and with his left hand he became a demon marble-player, winning so many marbles that by selling them he added substantially to his pocket money.

He became more and more interested in mechanical things – something engendered by his earlier and somewhat unwilling help demanded by his brothers on their jalopies – and built himself a bicycle out of bits and pieces.

'I remember inflating the tyres of my bicycle by holding the pump with the toes of my right foot against a spoke of the wheel and pumping with my left hand – excellent training for what was to come.'

When Phillip was eleven years old he learned to drive – clandestinely.

'My mother was hard of hearing so I could sometimes pull my brother's car in and out of the garage without her knowledge and when she was away with friends I tested my driving skills without interference,' Phillip admits. 'I knew my brother would never teach me so I stole his car in his absence.

'By the beginning of 1957 my brother had left home and my father developed lung cancer. On days when he felt very weak he asked me to drive to the outskirts of town where he took over. And the mechanical maintenance of the family car became my responsibility.

Since then Phillip has had a life-long love affair with driving and cars.

When Phillip's father died his mother sold the smallholding and moved with Phillip to a rented house in Krugersdorp. There in February, 1959, after swimming with friends he told his mother he felt very unwell. A doctor was called who diagnosed meningitis or poliomyelitis. In the Johannesburg Fever Hospital he was placed in an iron lung where he suffered terrible claustrophobia.

The medical staff explained to the fourteen-year-old that he would not be able to breathe outside the 'lung' but he pleaded so vigorously that the doctors finally agreed that if he could breathe on his own for three hours he could lie in a normal bed with a respirator attached to his chest.

of the machine was opened and Phillip was lifted out with nurses ready to rush him inside again if the experiment failed. Somehow the boy managed to breathe for six dramatic hours without help and the doctors' promise was kept. After that he managed to breathe for longer and longer periods until the chest respirator was discarded. It was only then that he began to realise that the other effect of the disease had been to paralyse his left arm.

In his impatient way Phillip felt driven to use his legs that were unaffected. After being fitted with a brace to support his lolling head, he was able to walk about though he had a problem of being off-balance with his single limp arm. However it was not long before he could use his feet to open doors and play cards with other patients.

His really difficult time came six months later when he was discharged from hospital and he went home where his mother looked after his physical needs.

'This was a bad time for me,' he recalls today. 'I could not go back to school and the only way I could read was to sit on the floor and turn the pages with my toes. I missed my father deeply but my sister Joey was always there to give us moral support.

Financially we never had much before but now things were worse. My mother, who was not healthy herself, had received little from the sale of the smallholding and only had a small pension. I started questioning my fate and my religious faith was tested to the utmost.'

'I felt very sorry for myself. What could a person without the use of their hands do? In those days many disabled people were an embarrassment, often hidden Away by their families. Yet the fact that my family surrounded me with love and encouragement did very little to pull me out of my despair.'

'I realise now it was not only a bad time for me – everybody around me was affected. I must have been a pain to others.'

At the end of this difficult year, Phillip entered Johannesburg's Hopes Home School, a special boarding school for handicapped children. Here the boy had an affinity with his disabled peers and made friends – and had fun. One problem was that he was the first disabled pupil without the use of his hands. It was decided that he might be able to type using a piece of dowel attached to a plastic mouthpiece, and the Olivetti company gave the school an electric typewriter for this purpose. This way Phillip was able to copy class notes.

A significant point in Phillip's life came in October, 1960, when the school's principal took him to the first exhibition of paintings mounted by the Association of Mouth and Foot Painting Artists in South Africa. There Erich Stegmann, the Association's founder, was introduced and Phillip was astonished by the way he did a quick portrait of one of the guests present.

The next day the AMFPA President visited the Hope Homes School and as Phillip was the only pupil there without hands one of the teachers suggested he might try to paint. While Stegmann watched he attempted a portrait with a mouth-held brush – a circle with three dots in it.

Recording that humble beginning, Phillip says,'Mr Stegmann became my role model. My aim was to do things the way he did. It was not easy but each little thing accomplished was a great personal victory to me.'

By the beginning of 1964 Phillip had completed his studies and returned to his mother's home and again he found it was not an easy time.

'Sometimes I got very frustrated when my mother was busy and I needed her to do something for me,' he says. 'I realise now how very wise she was. By not helping me, she actually forced me to do things for myself. Remembering Erich Stegmann, I sketched a lot.'

Next year some of Phillip's pictures were sent to be evaluated at the Association's head office in Liechtenstein with the result that he was accepted as a student.

This news was what Phillip describes as 'a new and purposeful life', he had a grant to pay for art lessons and real art materials – no longer did he have to paint on odd pieces of paper with any old pencil or crayon. Twice a week he travelled to Johannesburg to go to art classes.

'I drove myself harder and harder to learn as much as I possibly could,' Phillip says. 'I literally painted day and night and enjoyed every moment of it. Life had real meaning for me once again.

After two years, on the first of October 1967, I was granted full membership of the Association. I have been thanking God for Erich Stegmann ever since. Through his unselfishness I could have a new and wonderful life and dignity with it. And I know now without any doubt in my mind that God gave me a talent for painting when I needed it most.'

After Phillip had become a professional artist his fascination with cars returned and he drew plans showing how a car could be converted to be driven by a driver without hands. Helped by a friend, Cees Luyk, who was in the motor engineering business, Phillip converted a second-hand car and finally applied for a licence.

The request was so unusual that the test was conducted by a doctor, an engineer, a provincial traffic chief and his assistant. Phillip and his car were put through their paces for three hours in the grounds of a driving school with half the local population looking on. At the end of the test Phillip had qualified for a learner's licence.

Two weeks later a similar test took three-and-a-half hours and , not having made a single fault, Phillip came out with what he calls his 'licence to independence'.

It was also important for his painting because he was able to drive himself to distant places in search of landscapes that he would wish to capture on canvas. To date he has owned five cars and driven a total of 700,000 kms.

Another break-through came for Phillip in 1970 when a director of Africaans films offered him a part in a film.

'It told the story of a handful of mentally disturbed people and their life together in a private institution,' Phillip explains. 'I played the role of a physically disabled child who was hidden from the public eye in this asylum so as not to embarrass his rich parents. It was very challenging, especially as I was acting with some of the most able actors in South Africa. 'The money I earned from my work in this film enabled me to buy my first house so that for the first time mother and I could move out of rented accommodation.'

In 1978 Phillip experienced one of the happiest events in his life when he married his wife Cornelia who was then a secretary in the civil service. They still make a great team. When Phillip goes out to paint, Cornelia takes the photographs which enable him to complete his paintings in his studio at home. She travels thousands of kilometres with him each year when he goes on tour to give talks about the work of the Association, demonstrate foot painting and exhibit his work.

Of her husband Cornelia says, 'When Phillip decides to do something he will patiently struggle for hours until he is satisfied with the end result. But he can be impatient at times, I remember once how impatient he was cutting through a pipe using his foot to work the saw. When I asked him what the matter was, he said, "if only I had another pair of feet."

Living with Phillip is a rare experience. His independent, helpful and gallant nature makes life with him easier... and he still brings me flowers after all these years.'

Next to art Phillip's interest in cars continues and he is often approached by people who need advice and assistance in the designing and rebuilding of cars to suit their disabilities.

'Sometimes other disabled people just need somebody to talk to and it gives me great joy to be there for them,' he says. 'I have been through it already.'

Cristobal Moreno-Toledo

'All of life is beautiful.'

Many are the reasons that set a disabled person on the road to becoming an artist. It is something that might be suggested to pass the time in a hospital bed, it might be the desire to do something positive in a seemingly hopeless situation, it might be the sudden remembrance of a childish ambition – in the case of Cristobal Moreno-Toledo it was sparked by a boyish crush on a teacher.

Let us begin at the beginning. Cristobal Moreno-Toledo came into the world on 21 June 1941 in Castro del Rio in the province of Cordoba, Spain. Castro del Rio is renowned for its beauty and the fact that the author Miguel de Cervantes used it as a background for his novel *Don Quixote* – according to local legend he was imprisoned in the town when, as a collector of taxes, he fell foul of the Church. It is understandable that Cristobal has always loved his home town – the ambience that inspired Don Quixote to set forth to challenge the world also inspired him to tilt at the windmills of despair that can overshadow the disabled.

Until he was four years old Cristobal was like any other lively little boy but then his parents became aware of disquieting symptoms and progressive muscular dystrophy was diagnosed – the relatively rare disease that usually begins in childhood and continues to waste the muscles for up to twenty years, leaving the affected areas without the power of movement.

Doctors decided that the condition could be relieved by surgery. Each time the child was admitted to hospital there was an upsurge of hope, only to be dashed when it became clear that the operation had not been a success.

Before the disease deprived Cristobal of the use of his arms he was often seen racing in his wheelchair through the town's maze of winding streets in a way that could only be described as stylish. And style is something that he has retained down the years despite his disability.

Because of his condition following the operations he was forced to spend lonely hours at home with the result that, while his peers played football and enjoyed the mischief of boyhood, he retired into the world of the imagination and, to quote the writer Francisco Zueras, 'he used this time to develop his profound intellect'.

When Cristobal reached the age of thirteen he fell wildly in love with a schoolmistress and, eager to appreciate the things that were of importance to her, he developed a keen interest in literature. Here was something that had the power to carry him away from the world of the wheelchair on wonderful flights of fancy. The books he read inspired him with the idea of becoming an author, and the first requirement of a writer is to be able to physically write.

To this end Cristobal experimented with holding a pencil in his mouth and found that before long he was able to master the technique. It was then that he realized that if he could write he could also draw and his artistic career began. He entered into it with the enthusiasm that has been a characteristic of his life, teaching himself to paint everyday objects and scenes from the gentle landscape that surrounds his beloved town. Later he took a correspondence course with the Parramon Institute of Barcelona and, when he felt confident in the techniques of painting, he developed a distinctive style by generously applying colours with a mouth-held spatula.

It was while he was training himself to become an artist that he struck up a friendship with a young man named Javier Criado which was to trigger a turning point in Cristobal's life. The two shared many interests and their conversations on art were always a great pleasure and encouragement to the tyro. One day in 1962 Javier excitedly told him about a journal known as *Artis-Muti*, the official publication of an organisation devoted to the promotion of disabled artists, the Association of Mouth and Foot Painting Artists.

Prompted by his friend, Cristobal selected some of his drawings and had them sent off to the Association's office in Madrid where they were immediately dispatched to the Vaduz headquarters to be placed in an exhibition. In March 1963 he was awarded a scholarship and a mere eight months later he received the delightful news that he had been made a full member of the Association. From now on he could enjoy financial security and live a more comfortable life.

It was a significant year for the artist as his paintings appeared in more exhibitions and his work began to show Impressionist influences. From that time Cristobal has demonstrated his versatility. To look through a catalogue of his work one sees powerful studies of people – a beggar woman with her child, a reclining nude, a farmer riding his donkey, a late night procession – all come to life on his canvases. Then there are the still life studies of fruit, and fish laid out ready for the pot, and portraits which have a delicacy associated with crayons that are in contrast to his bold spatula-applied oils.

Turning from canvas and paper he created a series of mother-and-child studies on ceramic tiles, and he has also ventured into the field of modernistic sculpture, designing fantastic figures out of pieces of metal welded together. Of course it is impossible for him to do such work with his useless hands so he sits in his wheelchair while a technician cuts the metal to his directions.

In London he gained fame at an AMFPA exhibition in the Royal Festival Hall when he painted a lightning portrait of Nicholas Scott, the then Minister for the Disabled.

Such quick studies are one of his specialities but he took longer on a a large oil portrait of Pope John Paul II which he presented to His Holiness during an audience held for AMFPA members in St Peter's Church in Rome in 1992. He was given a Papal plaque as mark of esteem and Marlyse Tovae, President of the AMFPA, received a letter from a Vatican official, part of which read, '...may I kindly inform you that His Holiness has instructed me to convey to you sincere thanks... for the presentation of the painting by the Spanish artist Cristobal Moreno-Toledo. From his heart the Holy Father prays to God to protect and assist you, the esteemed members of the AMFPA and all those close to them.'

Since Cristobal began painting his work has been shown in over a score of collective exhibitions as well as in a similar number of one-man shows, examples of his art have been reproduced in an impressive book simply entitled *Cristobal Moreno-Toledo* together with essays on him by critics. One wrote: 'Above all, his paintings exude the expressive force which is the soul of the Cordoban countryside and its people. His work is a living testimony to his deep and sincere contemplation of life – there are no gimmicks and no pretensions.'

Cristobal has received many distinctions in his own country, France and USA. To be working at something one loves and to receive recognition for it is a great achievement for a man with no use in his limbs, yet it is not enough for for this quietly spoken artist with flowing hair and a goatee beard. There is also his art gallery...

In Castro del Rio stands a picturesque gateway with a tiled arch, wrought ironwork and a guardian statue of a figure in classical drapery. Beyond this is a gallery which Cristobal set up to exhibit the work of little know artists. It is called 'Mirazhara' which is based on the names of Cristobal's three daughters – Azahara, Elena and Myrian.

This artist has come along way since he first took a pencil between his teeth as a lonely boy but the vital spark of his creativity is still as bright as ever. He is a man who obviously loves life and he sums up his credo with the words, 'All of life is beautiful.'

Marlyse Tovae

'The world is so beautiful.'

In 1957, on an early spring day in Vaduz, Liechtenstein, a meeting took place which, although they then had no knowledge of it, was to alter the lives of hundreds of people around the world. The first General Meeting of the Association of Mouth and Foot Painting Artists had been called by its founder and first president Erich Stegmann, and was attended by sixteen disabled artists from eight European countries.

It was here, at the Hotel Waldorf, that the blueprint for the AMFPA was laid down and agreed, and in its statutes was this characteristic paragraph, 'The AMFPA adopts a neutral position from a religious, ideological and political point of view. Any preference or prejudice because of the religious, ideological or political beliefs of a member is not therefore permissible.'

Among the assembled artists was a young red-haired woman named Marlyse Tovae who, like the others, was excited by the thought of how the new-born Association would affect her, little dreaming of the effect that she would have on the Association some day.

The year of 1957 was a good one for Marlyse for not only had she been able to travel to Vaduz to be in at the inauguration of the co-operative that was to bring security to disabled artists like herself, but in France she had been awarded the silver medal of the Society for Art, Science and Literature which was sponsored by the then President of France René Coty. The honour was in recognition of her achievement as a painter despite the fact that she had been born without arms in Strasbourg in 1933.

As a young child using her feet she learned to put on her clothing, play with toys and feed herself with the ease of able-bodied children. Today, when the author enjoyed a supper with her in Vaduz, he found she was so graceful at using her foot as a hand that the other diners were hardly aware of any disability.

With such early skills going to school presented few problems, but when she was attending high school illness interrupted her studies.

One result of this was that while at home her interest in painting developed using pencils and brushes held between her toes. Her efforts were rewarded in the first year when she won first prize in an art competition. Encouraged by this, and in better health, she attended a private school run by the well known artist Marthe Kiehl and then Strasbourg's School of Fine Arts.

Talking to the author J.H. Rîesler when he interviewed her for his book *God's Second Door*, which was published in 1958, she told him, 'I am happy. I was always happy. I have tried to give a meaning to my life and I have succeeded. I have been painting since I was eighteen. Before that I was at a school of music. Mama wanted me to become a radio broadcaster but I love painting more than anything else. The world is so beautiful and all nature so perfectly planned, and I am just doing my little part so that people may see this.

'I have wonderful parents. The doctors advised my mother to put me in a home but Mama did not want that. She taught me to use my foot for the daily things – to take up a cup, to open a door, to eat my soup with a spoon. I never missed my arms.'

One of the most thoughtful things that Marlyse's mother did was to invite neighbourhood children to play in the garden so that her daughter would be used to the company of able-bodied children – and they to her – by the time she started school.

'They were all very charming to me,' Marlyse recalls. 'Each girl wanted to be my best friend and the boys fought each other for the privilege of carrying my schoolbag.'

KLAUS SPAHNI *Tulips* Watercolour 31 x 41 cm

KLAUS SPAHNI *Butterfly* Pencil 18 x 24 cm

KLAUS SPAHNI *Animus and Anima* Acrylic 90 x 116 cm

PHILLIP SWANEPOEL   *Flowers in the Desert*   Oil   22 x 30

PHILLIP SWANEPOEL   *Herding the Goats*   Oil   23 x 30 cm

Overleaf: PHILLIP SWANEPOEL   *Elephants*   Oil   41 x 51 cm

Phillip Swanepoel

PHILLIP SWANEPOEL   *Passing the Time*   Oil   30 x 40 cm

PHILLIP SWANEPOEL   *Bush Landscape*   Oil   40 x 50 cm

190

CHRISTOBAL MORENO TOLEDO *Girl with Umbrella* Oil

CHRISTOBAL
MORENO TOLEDO
Town in the South
Oil

CHRISTOBAL MORENO TOLEDO *Cortijo* Oil 46 x 55 cm

MARLYSE TOVAE
Sunflowers
Oil   80 x 64 cm

MARLYSE TOVAE
Ships at the Harbour
Oil   54 x 45 cm

MARLYSE TOVAE
Owl
Branded Wood 80 x 60 cm

MARLYSE TOVAE
Owl
Mosaic

194

MARLYSE TOVAE *River Bank* Watercolour 60 x 44 cm

JOSÉ URIBE   *Fruit & Flowers*   Watercolour   38 x 43 cm

JOSÉ URIBE   *Still Life with Fruits & Wine*   Oil

JOSÉ URIBE
Dome of the Cathedral in Compania
Watercolour   45 x 30 cm

JOSÉ URIBE   *Landscape outside Guanjuato*   Watercolour   32 x 45 cm

197

STOJAN ZAFRED
Flowers
Tempera   65 x 47 cm

STOJAN ZAFRED
Chimney
Oil   119 x 99 cm

STOJAN ZAFRED *Flowers* Watercolour 56 x 38 cm

STOJAN ZAFRED *Ready for Christmas*
Gouache   44 x 34 cm

In his book J. H. Rîesler described Marlyse's home which she had turned into a refuge for stray and injured animals – at that time there was a resident population of three dogs and five cats with a fluctuating number being nursed back to health. The attractive ones were then found suitable homes, Marlyse explaining, 'It is easy to be kind to the good-looking animals, the ugly and sick ones are better off with me.'

To misquote William Wordsworth, the Child is mother of the Woman!

After becoming one of the founder members of the AMFPA Marlyse continued her art career with unflagging enthusiasm. Landscapes, still life studies, portraits – all subjects were tackled, and having mobility, she was able to paint outdoors rather than copy from photographs.

A photograph in the AMFPA's archives shows her seated in a field in Ireland painting the famous Blarney Castle. Not only did she capture the castle on canvas but she kissed the Blarney Stone. This triangular stone is set high in the castle wall and is difficult to reach, in fact to kiss it the visitor has to be held by a custodian so that the upper half of his or her body is suspended over a dizzy drop. But the reward – so it is said – is the gift of beguiling speech. After meeting Marlyse one begins to believe there is truth in these old legends.

As an artist Marlyse has never been content to stand still, turning to pottery, metal work and large brilliantly coloured mosaics, each tiny piece being set in place with her remarkably sensitive foot. Latterly she has experimented with abstract painting.

When Erich Stegmann planned to set up an organisation by which mouth and foot painters would be able to support themselves through their ability to produce works that could be commercially reproduced he looked for artists who were already of a professional standard. Later, when the Association became viable, it would be possible to train disabled people who showed artistic talent through the scholarship system but the success of the venture depended on the efforts of those first pioneering members such as Marlyse, Erich Macho and the late Carl Fischer-Cefischer who are also mentioned in this book. And the Association benefited not only from Marlyse's painting ability but through her zest for the advancement of her fellow disabled painters.

In September 1984 Erich Stegmann died at the age of 72 years at Deisenhofen near Munich where he had rebuilt his publishing house after the Second World War. In June of the following year the Association's Board members met in Madrid where the main item on the agenda was the election of the new president.

It took almost five hours for the members to decide democratically who was to take on the mantle of the founder and when the vote was finally taken the majority of members elected Marlyse. The well-known English mouth painter Peter Spencer stood against her but as soon as the verdict was known he gave her a congratulatory kiss like the gentleman he was.

Next year in Vaduz the Association held a Jubilee meeting and art exhibition to celebrate its third decade of existence.

As president Marlyse declared, 'Thirty years ago, in the Principality of Liechtenstein, an organisation of artists from all over the world was formed. Today this organisation allows more than two hundred mouth and foot painting artists from all corners of the globe to enjoy a secure existence. Only someone who is physically handicapped himself can judge what it means to be largely independent of state assistance and social welfare: for most of us this is everything: life itself and personal freedom...'

Another decade has passed since then and the number of artists quoted by Marlyse has doubled.

Today Marlyse lives in Geneva where she continues to paint though her duties as President of the Association are now her main concern. When she was in her early twenties she declared, ' I have tried to give a meaning to my life.'

Since then, through her work with the Association, this pleasant quietly spoken woman has helped to give meaning to the lives of people who like herself have longed to become professional artists despite the fact that they could never hold a brush in the normal way.

José Gerado Uribe Aguayo

'Love is central to everything.'

At 8.30 on the morning of 16 March 1963 Rosa Maria Uribe Aguayo gave birth to a son in the city of Dolores Hidalgo in the state of Guanajuato in Mexico's central region. Before she was given the baby to hold she was warned that he was not normal, and when she took him she saw that he had been born without arms and his legs were deformed.

How had this catastrophe happened?

Rosa Maria believed that it was the result of medication taken during her pregnancy but this could not be proved. Whatever the cause, the fact remained that José Gerardo, as the child was christened, was severely disabled and in everyone's opinion could only look forward to a bleak future.

'From the very beginning my family felt that I would never be able to lead an adequate life,' José Gerardo told the author. 'They did not believe that I would ever be able to walk, eat or even move independently. They probably felt that I would always be a burden. My parents and my brothers had to carry me down the street as I always found it difficult to keep my balance because of the disproportionate length of my legs compared to the rest of my body.

'Inside the house I used to drag myself around on my bottom using my feet to propel me along.'

What must have affected the confidence of the child was the fact that he had three lively brothers and four equally lively sisters, and from an early stage the contrast between himself and his active siblings was painfully apparent to him.

It seemed that with everyone's mind made up that José's case was hopeless, no one thought of trying to improve it until he was four years old when his grandmother held him upright and tried to get him to take a step in the way that one would encourage a baby. After a while he did learn to take some stumbling steps and his Uncle Luis bought him a baby walker. At last he experienced the wonderful sensation of being able to move about the house on his own.

Two years later he no longer needed this help, he could walk by himself though he frequently fell over as his balance remained uncertain.

Just as it had been believed that José was incapable of walking, so it had been thought that it would be impossible for him to write or attend school. But after he had shown that he was capable of making progress his father put a pencil between the toes of his left foot and began teaching him to draw and form letters.

The director of a local school was highly impressed with the pictures José produced by this method and suggested to his parents that he should start going to school.

'My mother thought that it would be a good idea for me to learn to read as at least it would give me something to occupy myself with – after all, I was never going to be able to go out to work,' José recalls. 'On my first day at school my teacher did not want to accept me into his class as he was afraid that the children would give me a hard time. The headmaster finally persuaded him to take me in – and I found that my classmates treated me with respect and were always asking me questions about my situation.'

While José was happy to attend school, he found the break an unhappy time – with nobody to look after him he was unable to go out to play and had to watch his friends having fun from a distance.

José's mischievous' brother Juan Manuel also attended the school but was two years ahead of José. Each morning he would wheel him to school in a little cart and as he approached the gates, he broke into a run so that he charged through them at a dare-devil speed to the admiration of the pupils who waited for the display every morning – and to the terror of José.

'The fact that my brothers did not particularly want to help me gave me the advantage of having to learn to do everything myself,' José says.

In 1975 when José completed primary school, where he had become proficient at reading and foot-writing, he spent two years at the Institute of Rehabilitation in Mexico City. Here it was believed that his life could be improved by the fitting of mechanical arms, a project that was funded by the wife of the Governor of Guanajuato.

At first the boy was terrified that they would be grafted on to him by surgery making him part robot and he experienced a flood of relief when it was explained that such drastic treatment was not necessary. Although he 'wore' his artificial limbs while at the Institute they were not a success. José had become so adapt at using his feet that he found little benefit from them while on the other hand they were awkward, heavy and encroached on his sense of personal space. After his period at the Institute he gave up using them – thankfully.

While José was at the centre his ability at drawing was recognised and it was hoped that his mechanical hands would further his skill. Unfortunately they lacked the necessary flexibility and he continued to use his foot, copying sketches in order to master the technique of water colour painting.

'In the second year at the Institute I became increasingly mindful of my physical state because in Mexico City I could observe other people in similar situations to mine,' says José. 'I also started to think very deeply about philosophical matters – fate, the purpose of existence, the boundaries of being, the infinite...'

These thoughts awakened such an interest in philosophy that José determined to read the subject at the University of Guanajuato after completing his studies at preparatory college. It meant that he would have to leave his family and the support they provided but to José the need to learn more was paramount.

'Living in the city of Guanajuato was an incredible experience,' says José. 'I got to know a lot of friends and people who would prove very supportive. I grew further and further apart from my family and became completely immersed in my new environment. Guanajuato is very much a cultural centre and my university experience – I was enrolled at the School of Philosophy – gave me a new way of looking at things and my expectations began to change. There were so many opportunities to learn all kinds of subjects in this cultural hotbed and I took art classes with the teacher Jorge Rocha who instilled in me the principles of still life.'

For his degree thesis José wrote 'The Compositional Elements of Art' in which he set out the fundamentals of an aesthetic analysis of paintings which had developed from his own practical work. Now this interest in painting took over his life and after he completed his philosophical studies he took a course at the School of Creative Studies under the direction of Patricia Van Vloten. Here he learned the techniques of oil painting and colour blending and encaustic art – an ancient classical method of painting with coloured waxes and 'fixing' them by heat.

By now José was beginning to receive recognition for his efforts. In 1987 the President of Mexico, Miguel de La Madrid, presented him with the First National Youth Award in the Presidential Residence in Mexico City, and later he was to receive an accolade from a completely different quarter.

At the beginning of the Eighties he had learned of the Association of Mouth and Foot Painting Artists from the well-known Mexican foot painter Demetrio Herrera Olivares but he decided to work at his art until he felt it was of a satisfactory standard before approaching the organisation. In 1990 a selection of his work was parcelled up and sent to the AMFPA headquarters in Liechtenstein.

'I was accepted for a scholarship by the Association which meant that I could free myself from some of my obligatory activities, which I had to do to earn money, and concentrate on my creative output,' José says. 'If it was not for the financial backing afforded by the Association I would have found it very difficult to continue in my chosen occupation. It gave me the freedom to develop various techniques and I have been able to take courses in several different cities, some quite close such as San Miguel de Allende and Guanajuato and some further afield such as Madrid where I spent many months thanks again to the support of the Association.

'In March 1994 I became a full member of the Association. This has given a whole new direction to my life both artistically and personally and for this I am profoundly grateful.'

Today José lives in the city of his birth, Dolores Hidalgo, at the home of his family where he has a well-lit studio that is separate from the house. Here he works mostly in silence but sometimes with music providing a background. Like the author of this book he prefers the music of Vangelis to work to 'because no two records of his are ever alike'.

'Like him, it is important to me that all of my canvasses are different from one another,' he declares. 'I try to communicate a sense of order and a certain harmony or equilibrium in the forms represented. Some of my work has been influenced by religious images and constructions. City churches are remarkable edifices. They exude a stability of form underlined by the recurrence of adornments and the dynamic concept of my work is inspired by the on-going dialogue between straight lines and curves, all in carved stone.

'I also work with still life and one of my favourite themes involves those objects associated with eating and drinking – bottles, bread and fruit. I also like to combine different objects such as a violin, a vase and a swatch of cloth.

'Landscapes also fascinate me, mountains especially. Flat lands leave me cold, as do the new towns that have wiped out the old urban landscape. However, the human figure is the greatest inspirer with all its different postures, proportions and textures.'

For José the production of a painting begins with him listening to music in order to create an aura of tranquillity and, after arranging the model of the subject he is about to draw, he sits and regards it for a couple of hours, pondering on the elements of composition it will need such as colour, light and atmosphere.

The next day he outlines the subject with a small brush and then begins work on the background, experimenting with a colour until he achieves exactly the right shade he is looking for.

'The first attempt at a background is never the definitive one,' he explains. 'I still have to elaborate more thoroughly on whatever objects there are in the distance. Each object must acquire its own importance and contribute to the whole. My work always develops gradually, piece by piece. It can take me several sessions of five or six hours at a time to finish a canvas.

'I tend to work mostly with oils though I use water colours for expressiveness and pencil drawing if I want to create something more direct. I prefer to work with natural light and so I always paint in the mornings when the tones and hues of objects are most enhanced.'

An unusual thing about José as a foot painter is that he uses his mouth as well, mainly to fill in backgrounds because that way he can cover a large area more quickly. But the detailed work is always done with a brush held in his toes as the foot allows him more flexibility.

In speaking about his handicap today this versatile artist says, 'Physical disability can be a strong impediment and it is possible to fall into the trap of trying to shield oneself from the world. To avoid this feeling of limitation or lack of confidence it is essential to maintain contact with friends and to take on a larger view of the world. The best thing is to maintain one's own independence as completely as possible – after all, I can't look to other people to create a canvas for me.

'The thing I value above all else is the companionship of friends. It is so important to spend time with those you love and to be able to share your worries and the things that make you happy. Love is central to everything and it is love that inspires the colours and forms I use in my art.'

Stojan Zafred

'The Paintbrush guided by the Heart'

Stojan Zafred is one of several members of the AMFPA who became disabled through diving accidents. In each case the victim was full of youthful vitality and in a matter of moments condemned to the wheelchair for life. Stojan was no exception. It was the day before his nineteenth birthday, and in the age of Rock music he was a member of a band and saw his future as a musician. Then, as he himself puts it, he 'dived into a different world full of the unknown.'

Stojan was born in 1951 in Postojna, Slovenia, which until 1991 had been part of Yugoslavia. His late father Franc was a telephonist with the state railway company and his mother Marija is a housewife, the rest of the family being made up Stojan's sisters Sonja, Magda and Vlasta. The children were very fond of music and singing, reflecting the taste of their father who was a member of the local wind band.

'This sincere feeling for music influenced the whole period of my youth,' says Stojan. 'I also remember very clearly my first painting lesson in my elementary school. To me it was an event which I very often connect with my enthusiasm for music – at that moment I felt a strong link between melody and colour, and in this link I always find my joy of painting.'

When Stojan was ten years old his father took him to the local bandmaster, he was given a trumpet to learn and several years later he joined an orchestra. After finishing elementary school he was enrolled as a boarder in the Technical High School in Ljubljana where his father hoped he would graduate as an electrical technician.

Looking back on that time he recalls that he sometimes had tears in his eyes when he felt homesick, the boarding school seemed an alien place and coupled with this was the fact that he had little interest in electrical engineering.

'I was too involved with music,' he explains. 'I realized I was not born to be a technician and just before my final exam I stopped studying in order to play the music in which I saw my future.

'On 12 July 1970 I joined a group of friends to go swimming. We dived into water from a height of five or six metres. The water turned out to be very shallow and my dive ended with the accident. In a blink I was born again.'

In hospital Stojan heard the doctors talking in low tones about tetraplegia but he did not know the meaning of the word. In reality he had broken a cervical vertebra which meant that his arms, hands and legs would remain paralysed for life. It was when he looked up into the faces of his relatives that he realized that nothing could ever be the same as before, everything he had been looking forward to was gone and he would have to start life again from the very beginning.

In a letter to the author Stojan wrote: 'Lying immobile and staring at the whiteness of the hospital room and the gowns of the attendants aroused an unknown energy deep in my personality. Some might call it "life energy", others simply "God".

'I have often been asked how I started as a painter. For me it was very simple. I just knew I had to live. There was no other choice. I tried to continue the things I dealt with in my previous life – the will to create still remained.

'In hospital my sister was the first to put a pencil in my mouth. My early letters looked clumsy but my first drawing was not so bad. The impossible became the possible though I have a feeling that for the majority of people my first experiments in painting were more funny than anything else.'

Exactly two years after his tragic dive, when he was in residence at the Institute of Rehabilitation, friends gave Stojan a set of oil paints. He had started with pencil drawings and then moved on to felt pens but at that time he knew nothing about oils or turpentine. Trial and error was the method by which he learned and, as he had always had an affinity with animals, his first subject was a dog, followed by similar pictures. Before long he had enough oil paintings to hold an exhibition and this convinced the Institute authorities that he was serious in his desire to become a painter.

After two years in the Institute Stojan returned home to find that after living with people who had the shared problem of disability it was difficult to adjust to the world of the able-bodied. He became conscious of being different from others and he had to face traumas and depression which were eventually overcome thanks to an inbuilt optimism and enthusiasm for painting.

Stojan declares that after his initial experiments with painting at the Institute his real life began back in Karst, the region where he was born. Here new horizons opened as he became aware of things he had never considered before. He painted traditional stone cottages and landscapes, and in his paintings he sought to preserve what he felt was a world vanishing before the effects of modern civilization.

In 1972 Stojan had his first one-man public exhibition in Postojna which was organized by friends and old schoolmates. It was a great moment in his life as it was visited by journalists, critics and well-known professional painters. One of the journalists, Evgen Juric, wrote an article which he aptly entitled 'The Paintbrush guided by the Heart', and he also introduced Stojan to a famous woman painter named Seka Tavcar who became his mentor and guided him in the techniques of oil, gauche and watercolour painting.

His next exhibition, in 1974, was in Divca the town where he now lives.

'Now I felt the dive that had rushed me into a wheelchair had carried me on to a world of great richness and the depressions I suffered became less and less,' he says. 'Often friends sent me postcards that were reproductions of works by mouth and foot painting artists and that is how I found out about that AMFPA, the unique family of those who in spite of physical disability live independent lives.

'In 1976 I submitted some of my paintings to the Association's head office in Liechtenstein and was granted a scholarship. The financial support that followed meant that I no longer had to worry about finding money to buy brushes, paints and canvases. It was the beginning of my independence and as a result I felt more relaxed when I was working.

'In 1979 I had some health problems that forced me to return to the Institute for Rehabilitation and there I met my wife Jozica. It was another turning point for me. We were married in the October of that year and we able to move into a new apartment.

'About this time I recognized that I was becoming discontented with realistic painting and I began to experiment with new forms of expression, working on big canvasses with apocalyptic visions of vanishing Karst. Perhaps these pictures were a warning to those who were destroying the harmony that had been passed down from our ancestors – or perhaps it was a reflection of my own spiritual condition. Nevertheless there was a little light in those dark paintings as a symbol of hope.'

These paintings have a remarkable impact, being half realistic and half surreal studies of once picturesque places falling into decay. Painted in sombre colours, they are like a lament for a lost but innocent world. Today Stojan's visions of ghostly figures – people and animals – set in fantastic landscapes have the dreamlike elements of surrealistic art.

'I began to feel the spiritual aspect of the paintings,' Stojan says. 'It was God who was more and more present in them. Before my fateful dive it seemed to me that God had always been moving away into some abstract horizon. My parents had been educated in the spirit of Christianity but the main characteristic of my education was the confrontation of two opposing global ideologies – Christianity and communism.

'This ideological conflict meant that in some respects I felt more at home at school than with my family, but now I know that the accident had made it possible for me to recognize my God in an entire way – something I felt in the form of life energy. I could not connect it with any religious group – it was completely my own religion – but that did not worry me because I started to feel a powerful inner light and I dare to claim that this is reflected in my works.'